BEST SUMMIT HIKES
DENVER to VAIL

BEST SUMMIT HIKES
DENVER TO VAIL
HIKES AND SCRAMBLES ALONG THE I-70 CORRIDOR

JAMES DZIEZYNSKI

WILDERNESS PRESS . . . *on the trail since 1967*

Best Summit Hikes Denver to Vail: Hikes and Scrambles Along the I-70 Corridor

Copyright © 2016 by James Dziezynski

Published by Wilderness Press

Distributed by Publishers Group West

Printed in the United States of America

First edition, first printing

Cover design: Scott McGrew

Book design: Lisa Pletka and Annie Long

Maps: © National Geographic Maps, with trails added by the author

All cover and interior photos, except where noted, by James Dziezynski

Front cover photos: (top) Reaching the summit of Drift Peak (see page 140); (bottom) looking west to Vail Pass and the Gore Range from Jacque Peak (see page 145)

Back cover photos: (background) Summit of Mount Eva; author photographed by Jenny Salentine

Frontispiece: Sunset from Shrine Mountain, looking out on the Tenmile Range (see page 155). Left to right are Peak 10, Crystal Peak, and Pacific Peak. Photographed by Wendy Cranford.

Library of Congress Cataloging-in-Publication Data

Names: Dziezynski, James.

Title: Best summit hikes Denver to Vail : hikes and scrambles along the I-70 corridor / James Dziezynski.

Description: First edition. | Birmingham, AL : Wilderness Press, [2016] | "Distributed by Publishers Group West"—T.p. verso. | Includes webography and index.

Identifiers: LCCN 2016007499| ISBN 9780899978116 | ISBN 9780899978123 (EISBN)

Subjects: LCSH: Hiking—Colorado—Denver Metropolitan Area—Guidebooks. | Hiking—Colorado—Vail Region—Guidebooks. | Trails—Colorado—Denver Metropolitan Area—Guidebooks. | Trails—Colorado—Vail Region—Guidebooks. | Interstate 70—Guidebooks. | Denver Metropolitan Area (Colo.)--Guidebooks. | Vail Region (Colo.)—Guidebooks.

Classification: LCC GV199.42.C62 D463 2016 | DDC 796.5109788/83—dc23

LC record available at https://lccn.loc.gov/2016007499

 WILDERNESS PRESS
An imprint of AdventureKEEN
2204 First Ave. S, Ste. 102
Birmingham, AL 35233

Visit wildernesspress.com for a complete listing of our books and for ordering information. Contact us at our website, at facebook.com/wildernesspress1967, or at twitter.com/wilderness1967 with questions or comments. To find out more about who we are and what we're doing, visit our blog, blog.wildernesspress.com.

SAFETY NOTICE: Although Wilderness Press and the author have made every attempt to ensure that the information in this book is accurate at press time, they are not responsible for any loss, damage, injury, or inconvenience that may occur to anyone while using this book. You are responsible for your own safety and health while in the wilderness. The fact that a trail is described in this book does not mean that it will be safe for you. Be aware that trail conditions can change from day to day. Always check local conditions and know your own limitations.

Contents

Looking north down to I-70 from the high slopes of Republican Mountain (see page 33)

Dedication

*For Sheila. To be in the mountains with you . . . or anywhere at all . . .
is my favorite place in the world.*

In loving memory of Cynthia Cline.

And in honor of Colorado's greatest mountain dog, Sopris. Good girl, you can rest now.

photographed by Paul Lenhart

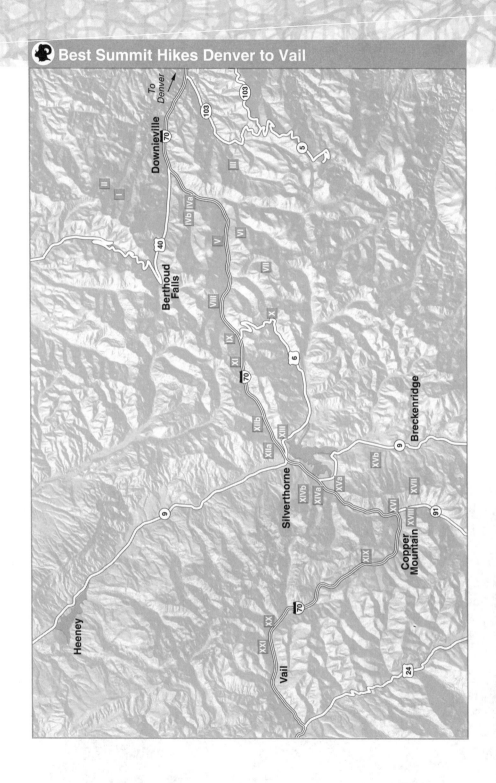

List of Trailheads

Diff.	Exit	
-6	238	I. Loch Lomond Trailhead (p. 12)
6	238	II. Fall River Reservoir Trailhead (p. 18)
5	240	III. West Chicago Creek Trailhead (p. 26)
3-6	232	IV. Empire–Republican Mountain Trailhead and Bard Creek Trailhead (p. 31)
6,5	226	V. Silver Plume–7:30 Mine Trailhead (p. 39)
5	228	VI. Waldorf Mine Trailhead (p. 46)
4	221	VII. Stevens Gulch Trailhead (p. 55)
6-8	218	VIII. Herman Gulch Trailhead (p. 62)
6,5	216	IX. Dry Gulch Trailhead (p. 72)
4	216	X. Loveland Pass Trailhead (p. 80)
5-6	NA	XI. Loveland Tunnel West Trailhead (p. 88)
5-6	205	XII. Ptarmigan Peak Trailhead and Laskey Gulch Trailhead (p. 100)
5	205	XIII. Tenderfoot Mountain Trailhead (p. 106)
3-6	205	XIV. Meadow Creek Trailhead and Ryan Gulch Trailhead (p. 111)
8	201	XV. Peak 1 Trailhead and Miners Creek Trailhead (p. 121)
3	195	XVI. Far East Trailhead (p. 128)
7-9	195	XVII. Mayflower Gulch Trailhead (p. 132)
7	195	XVIII. Copper Mountain/Spaulding Gulch Trailhead (p. 143)
2-4	190	XIX. Vail Pass Trailhead and Gore Range Copper Trailhead (p. 150)
10	180	XX. Deluge Lake Trailhead (p. 156)
8	180	XXI. Pitkin Creek Trailhead (p. 163)

Acknowledgments

My heartfelt thanks to all those who were part of the adventure. Your encouragement, good cheer, and enthusiasm mean the world to me.

Mountains of Thanks

To Sheila Powell—without you, the mountains are just big rocks. Thank you for your love and support both on and off the trail.

On the Trail

My golden boot awards (are those a real thing?) go out to David Tanguay, Jenny Salentine, Meredith "She's the Cooniest!" Knauf, Dany Tanguay, Paul Retrum, Richard Harvey, Bart Deferme, Jayme Moye, Paul Lenhart, Lindsey Tate, Katie D'Amelio, Dr. Jon Kedrowski, and Kyle Sevits.

Canine Accolades

To my own pups, Mystic and Fremont, mountain companions without equal—good boys! Also Hayduke (for putting up with Hells Hole), Watanga and Agnes (for their inspiration), Clyde (who has developed into a top-notch mountain dog), Maizey (border collie extraordinaire), Lucy (my birthday buddy), and Sherlock (the wiggle that won the West). And a feline shout-out to Xanadu, my cat-o-grapher and companion on many late writing nights.

Behind the Scenes

Thanks to Wilderness Press—this book would literally not be possible without you! Also Ron Pratt, David and Lynne Dziezynski, Janet Seston, Amy and Michael Karls, Candice Blodgett, Doug Schnitzspahn, Lou Dzierzak, Fynn Glover and the RootsRated crew, Sarah Leone, and Mary Anne Potts.

Extra Special Thanks

Jon Bradford for your guidance, mountain expertise, and friendship over the years. Chris Tomer, thanks for all the forecasts! Emily Gillis for taking such wonderful care of the pets. Melanie Moffat, thanks for letting the pups crash with you when they couldn't be in the mountains. Evelyn Pinney, for your support and help on the Vail front. Jennifer and John Danese, for insider's info in the Frisco region. Also Jay Getzel and the Mountainsmith crew and Garmin for GPS equipment and technical help.

And finally, thanks to all those people whose names I may have missed. You know who you are—and apparently I don't.

Introduction

This book exists because of a simple philosophical query: "What happens if I go right instead of left?"

In this case, *right was a turn toward enigmatic Watrous Gulch;* left was the weary path to the beautiful but busy Herman Lake. The seldom-traveled trail to Watrous Gulch eventually gives up altogether, dissolving into a green field of dazzling wildflowers. At its terminus is an amphitheater watched over by a trio of inviting mountains, all blissfully void of established trails.

These places awaken something in me. Troubles fade away in sync with the quieting traffic on I-70, not even a mile and a half down the trail but already light-years away. Focus shifts away from mundane routine toward the thrilling unknown.

My border collie Fremont and I linked up Mount Parnassus, Bard Peak, Robeson Peak, and Engelmann Peak on that day. Standing atop the highest point at 13,641-foot Bard Peak, I saw summits to the east—Silver Plume Mountain and Republican Mountain—that I had never hiked. I began to realize a wealth of great summit hikes potentially waiting along the I-70 corridor. Most of these relatively unknown mountains are gone in a flash, overlooked as eager adventurers drive to far-off, more-popular peaks. Given how wonderful my day out of Watrous Gulch had been, I began to give serious merit to the low-traffic, high-adventure mountains lining the I-70 corridor like open secrets.

And with that, this book was afoot.

It's not that the entire suite of I-70 peaks between Denver and Vail are completely anonymous. The twin fourteeners of Grays and Torreys Peaks are among the most heavily trafficked mountains in all of Colorado. But what about Tenderfoot Mountain? Mount Solitude? Hagar Mountain? Uneva Peak? Peak 6? How about all those mountains that fatigued drivers have looked upon while trapped in gridlock, wondering if they even have names?

This book is the culmination of more than five years of touring and exploring those very mountains. Perhaps it was a trick of perception, but they just seemed to be getting better along the way. An organic transformation happens east to west as the accommodating peaks of the Front Range slowly morph into the wild and untamed mountains of the magical Gore Range. That so many excellent hikes and scrambles near to the Denver–Boulder metro area go unnoticed is astounding. They are yours to uncover.

It is my hope that you find as much adventure, challenge, and enjoyment in these mountains as I have—hopefully more. I've purposely left some secrets out of print: wildflower meadows, old mining haunts, prime wildlife habitats, secret monuments, to name a few. I believe that a good guidebook will get you to the top and back safely but leave plenty of space between the lines for imagination and discovery.

After all, each step into the wilderness reveals something about the mountain—and about ourselves. And let's face it: It's awfully convenient that all of that enlightenment is waiting so close to home.

The roughly 70 miles of paved highway that connects Denver to Vail is an engineering marvel. Cutting through some of Colorado's highest terrain, I-70 goes 1.7 miles through the earth via the 11,158-foot Eisenhower–Johnson Memorial Tunnel and over 10,662-foot Vail Pass. Along the way, it passes through several distinct mountain ranges (all subranges of the Southern Rocky Mountains), including the Front Range, the Williams Fork Mountains, the Tenmile Range, and the Gore Range.

I-70 is the critical foundation upon which Colorado's thriving outdoors recreation industry is built. The highway is maintained year-round, offering access to several ski areas and tourism-based mountain towns. At times it is easy to forget just how amazing this roadway is, especially when you are mired for hours in the notorious gridlock that inevitably builds up in busy and winter months. On the plus side, it does give an aspiring adventurer plenty of time to gaze at the mountains.

The hikes in this book are divided into three primary sections: Denver to the Eisenhower–Johnson Tunnel, the tunnel to Vail Pass, and Vail Pass to the town of Vail. In order to narrow the focus, the rule for this book is that all trailheads are within 10 miles of an I-70 exit. A few bonus hikes just beyond this radius are given a quick look as well. Thankfully, nearly all of the trailheads for the peaks in this guide are accessible by any standard car or truck. Only four of the primary trailheads require a high-clearance, four-wheel-drive vehicle, and in all of those cases, stock SUVs tend to do just fine.

Colorado hikers are getting the best of both worlds hiking along I-70. It only takes 20 minutes to leave behind the droning buzz of traffic. Because so many of these mountains are overlooked, many hiking days are uncrowded, peaceful experiences. Yet, one is never far from civilization. From Denver, the farthest-west hikes are only about a 2-hour drive from home. The towns along the way have great restaurants and plenty of attractions to tack onto a good hiking day.

These mountain adventures are perfect for those who cherish time in the hills but only have so many days where they can get out. In no way are these peaks compromised in terms of quality or challenge—you are getting the real deal, minus the hassle of long drives along remote mountain roads. It is a happy coincidence that the terrain ranges from simple, on-trail walk-ups (Grays Peak) to burly, gutsy scrambles (Pacific Peak, west ridge).

Note on I-70 Tolls

At the time of writing, Colorado was enacting a new toll system for brief, heavily trafficked sections of I-70. Started in autumn 2015, a single toll lane (with varying costs) was opened to complement the free I-70 lanes. Travel on the highway remains toll-free, with the toll lane option for those in a hurry or sick of being stuck in traffic. Whether this strategy succeeds will be seen.

About This Guidebook

The rule for selecting peaks is that their **primary trailheads must be within 10 miles of the I-70 corridor.** In most cases, they are much closer than that.

While there are no technical routes requiring ropes or specialized mountaineering skills, there are some scrambles that have dangerous sections. Please read the class rating system on page 9 for more information.

One of the great things about this collection of mountains is that they can be combined in many different ways, especially as point-to-point adventures (which are easier to set up, since many of the trailheads are right along the highway).

While this guide mentions many of the possible route combinations, those looking for multiday adventures or huge single-day outings will find enough information to create unique routes.

All GPS tracks are available online in the GPX and KMZ file formats at mountainouswords.com/I70-hikes. These are free downloads for your personal use; please do not upload them on other sites.

While all the routes in this book are worthy (I've weeded out the stinkers), the very best are denoted by a star icon ✪. Consider these the must-do hikes!

Gear

Preparing for mountain hiking means that you may be dealing with blistering heat and frigid storms—sometimes in the same day! For three-season hiking in Colorado, here's a checklist of recommended gear.

It's been my experience that two particular pieces of gear are worth investing in the best possible options you can: **eye protection and footwear.** This doesn't necessarily mean the most expensive, but it does usually mean paying a bit more for better quality.

- High-quality footwear. I prefer a low-hiker with a rugged, Vibram outsole, often paired with gaiters for off-trail terrain. For off-trail hiking, a stiffer, full hiking boot is recommended for those with foot or ankle issues.
- High-quality eye protection. Make sure glasses cover your full range of eyesight and are UVA–UVB protected (without distortion from cheap lenses). I often pack along eye drops to use during and after the hike as well.
- First aid kit *(see page 5 for more details)*
- Noncotton base layers
- Lightweight rain/wind shell
- Lightweight, long-sleeved fleece
- Lightweight down or synthetic puffy jacket
- Gloves
- Winter hat and neck gaiter
- Visor or baseball cap
- Sunblock
- Camelbak *(or similar hydration system)* and at least 48 ounces of water
- Plenty of easy-to-digest food and snacks (I often use gels, gummies, and energy bars only on many hikes)
- 1,800- to 2,500-cubic-inch backpack
- Compass, map, GPS, or navigation-based smartphone app
- Gaiters
- Hiking poles *(strongly recommended for many of the hikes in this guide!)*

Safety: First Aid and Hiking at Altitude

The Effects of Altitude and Altitude Sickness

Lower levels of oxygen at altitude (more than 8,000 feet) affect people differently. Even fit, experienced hikers can have an off day due to altitude-related fatigue. It's important to know thyself—a worsening headache, lack of concentration, upset stomach, and elevated fatigue are all signs of mild AMS (acute mountain sickness). AMS can turn serious if not dealt with, even at Colorado's modestly low elevations (relatively speaking).

Of course, the tricky question here is this: How do I know if I'm experiencing AMS or just the inevitable fatigue of climbing a mountain?

A slightly dull headache is very common and isn't necessarily cause to turn around. Fast-acting ibuprofen (such as Advil Liqui-Gels) can stave off such headaches. Remember, a lot of people (this author included) wake up earlier than normal to hike, plus driving has a weariness all of its own. Preventative medication is common, especially when you know mountain hiking may aggravate your knees or back.

Nearly all hikers lose a bit of power at altitude, especially over 11,500 feet. Brief shortness of breath is expected. Steady hiking, with well-paced rests, is the way to go.

There are telltale signs of legit AMS however; these include the following:

- Change in personality and enthusiasm; irritability, indifference, or sudden silence should be noted.

- Extreme fatigue, as evidenced in slumped-over positions while resting.

- Vacant eyes, confusion, and slow comprehension.

- Sudden pounding headache and intense light sensitivity, often with nausea.

- Prolonged coughing.

Those suffering from these conditions should descend immediately (and if possible they should not be left to descend alone). Most altitude-related symptoms will (mercifully) go away when returning to lower elevations, sometimes as little as a thousand vertical feet. If symptoms do not clear up within 2–3 hours after returning to low altitude, seek medical attention.

The occasional randomness of AMS is one of the many good reasons it's worth hiking with trusted partners who know you well enough to notice significant changes in your personality—and vice versa. As someone who values hiking solo, I put extra emphasis on "checking in" with my body more often on adventures where I am by myself.

Preparing for high-altitude hikes isn't something that happens overnight. If I've been out of the mountains more than a month, I work my way back up to them by undertaking lower summits or easier days between 8,000 and 11,000 feet to get my body back in shape. Fitness does play a role in AMS, as does one's mental state. If you know how a steep trail feels at 9,000 feet, then you won't be alarmed if you feel the same fatigue at 13,000 feet.

In general, those living above 5,000 feet can visit the high peaks as day hikes with little trouble. Be especially aware when you have friends coming to town from sea level—let them work up to the bigger mountains!

First Aid Kit

A good first aid kit should be packed to address the common types of illnesses and injuries on mountain hikes. Because hiking at altitude tends to have regular medical issues, here's a look at what should be in your first aid kit:

- Painkillers (ibuprofen, acetaminophen, aspirin)—These will get a lot of use, so make sure you are stocked up both for yourself and your hiking companions/others you meet on the trail!
- Antacids—chewable Tums can help with altitude-related sour stomach.
- Blister pads and medical tape
- Adhesive bandages of various sizes (especially knuckle/finger size)
- Butterfly bandages
- Medical scissors
- Antibiotic ointment
- Sterile pads (two medium, two large)
- Alcohol pads
- Roller bandages
- Body thermometer
- Sugar packets/sugar candies
- Feminine sanitary pads
- Rubber gloves
- Sterile tweezers
- Syringe to wash out wounds
- Safety pins
- Plastic bags
- Foam-lined aluminum splint (such as a SAM splint)
- Laxatives
- Pen and paper (to record vitals/accident info)
- Sunscreen and lip balm
- Hand warmers
- CPR mask
- Small knife or multitool
- Energy gels
- Small LED flashlight
- Eye drops
- Burn cream

In addition, those with known allergic reactions to bees should carry an epinephrine pen.

Mountain Weather

Reading mountain weather is an art that is often practiced but never mastered. The best way to avoid storms is to start early (4–6 a.m., or earlier if you can) and be off all summits by 11 a.m. at the latest. Even with a perfect forecast, hikers should expect thunderstorms every day between May and September around 1 p.m. A barometer is useful to track incoming weather; in a very general sense, a dropping barometer means storms are brewing, while a rising barometer means the sky is clearing.

Just because storms regularly come in after noon does NOT mean they cannot develop earlier in the day. In June 2015, with a clear forecast, 15 people were injured when a bolt struck Mount Bierstadt shortly after 11 a.m. Thunderstorms are not to be trifled with. If there is already lightning and thunder before 10 a.m., it's best to come back another day. Storms can grow in a matter of minutes. I've seen pristine blue sky shift to violent storms in under 15 minutes at all times of the day.

Autumn is a fantastic time to hike, especially mid-September–mid-October. Storms are less likely to develop, the weather is cooler, and the change of seasons means fewer people on the mountains (though most hikes in this guide are already low traffic).

Be aware of the forecast for the day, and keep an eye for building thunderheads, which rise up in great, puffy columns with a dark bottom. Also, even in midsummer, a day can go from hot to cold in a flash—make sure you have enough clothes in your pack for chilly conditions.

Nutrition and Hydration

Over the years, I've developed a system that makes sure I stay hydrated and well fed throughout the day. I try to take in 100–200 calories per hour (usually in the form of gels or gummies) and drink small sips of water every 15–20 minutes. I often have plenty of water left over after hikes, but it beats the alternative. I take 48–90 ounces of water, depending on the length and difficulty of the day.

With food, I've found my performance is greatly improved when I avoid breads, bagels, and other carb-heavy foods while on the trail. Protein-based food (nuts, salmon, energy bars) is what your body craves and is easier to digest on the move.

One mistake many, many hikers make—even very experienced hikers—is they don't eat and drink enough on descents. While the hardest part of the day may be over, remain vigilant with your food (and sunscreen!) until the hike is done. A lot of people get dehydrated on the descent because they aren't sweating as much, but rest assured your body is burning through its water even when you are standing still!

GPS and Cell Reception

GPS is a wonderful tool. The affordability and ubiquitousness of smartphone apps mean there is little excuse to not have GPS on your side. I strongly consider investing in a handheld, dedicated GPS unit (such as the Garmin Oregon 650t, used in this book) if you plan to undertake off-trail hikes. If you do prefer to use a smartphone app, make sure it's one that can work in airplane mode to conserve battery life.

Because many of the hikes in this guide are well within cell phone range, chances are you'll have reception in a lot of places. Cell communication is a nice backup for emergencies, but don't count on it being reliable (especially the farther west you go). If you're planning on heading into the deep wilderness in the Gore Range or do a lot of solo hiking, consider an emergency locator device such as the DeLorme inReach, which will get a satellite lock nearly anywhere in the wilderness.

And as many a crusty, old hiker would lament, be competent with a compass and map. When technology fails, the magnetic field of the earth remains the champion of uptime.

All the GPS tracks used in this book are available online for free use at mountainouswords.com/I70-hikes and are available in the .gpx and .kmz formats.

Hiking with Dogs

Hiking with dogs may be my favorite way to explore the mountains, but it is a big responsibility. There are a lot of opinions on what terrain is acceptable for dogs, especially since every dog is different. Here are some general rules for hiking with your canine pals:

- Please obey all leash laws in wilderness areas. They are there for the safety of your dog as much as they are for the wildlife.

- If your dog isn't good with other hikers or dogs, keep them on leash (or seek out quieter hikes).

- Make sure you have more than enough food and water for your dog. I generally bring along an extra 48–80 ounces for my two dogs and top off my personal water to 100 ounces. Likewise, I make sure they have some healthy, yummy treats and make a point to feed them whenever I snack.

- Account for your dog by adding pet-specific items to your first aid kit. This includes pet wrap, needle-nose pliers (for thorns, porcupine quills, and so on), emergency blanket, paw wax (for heat or snow), and extra food. Additionally, a bear bell on the collar is a keen idea. Make sure your pups have some sort of orange vest or marking during hunting season.

My personal policy: Never take dogs on terrain harder than Class 2. There is no value in putting them in needlessly dangerous situations, even when they are physically capable. It's irresponsible to project your climbing ego onto your dog. Save the Class 1 and 2 adventures for them—there are plenty in this book!

And finally, if your dog says it's time to turn around . . . it's time to go home, no questions asked.

Please consult the appendix on page 174 for a list of veterinary clinics along the I-70 corridor.

How to Use This Book

Rather than address each individual peak with its own chapter, hikes in this book are arranged by trailheads. Because some of these trailheads offer access to the same peaks, it's good to have options to explore new routes on the same mountain. In each trailhead listing, peaks that appear for the first time will appear in a list, while peaks already covered in previous chapters will be listed in parentheses. A good example of this is Torreys Peak, which can be accessed by Stevens Gulch, Waldorf Mine, and Loveland Pass (among others).

The upshot means you'll have lots of great options at many of the trailheads. A weekend car-camping adventure to Mayflower Gulch can snag you Drift Peak, Atlantic Peak, Pacific Peak, Crystal Peak, and Mayflower Hill. Or you could even traverse over from Crystal Peak and do a point-to-point to the Colorado Trailhead at Copper Mountain. The ability to mix and match peaks is part of the allure of I-70's summit collection.

Driving Directions

While most of the driving directions are straightforward, extra attention has been paid to the legality of parking areas and accurate mileage counts. It can be infuriating when you wait all week for a great hike, just to get flustered by shoddy directions. All these hikes have been personally climbed by myself (often several times) and driving notes are of special note for accuracy.

Vehicle Recommendations

For each trailhead, vehicle recommendations are made. The majority of trailheads are reachable by passenger car. If not, roads are declared passable by sport-utility cars (SUCs) such as Subaru Outbacks/Honda CR-Vs, sport-utility vehicles (SUVs) like Toyota 4Runners/Nissan Xterras, or dedicated four-wheel-drive vehicles like modified Jeep Wranglers. If a road gets close to the trailhead before hitting a tough four-wheel-drive section, passenger car parking is provided.

While I now have a mountain-worthy vehicle, I spent many years exploring the mountains of Colorado in a beat-up Honda Accord and did pretty well! I-70 is especially accommodating for less burly vehicles.

Difficulty and Class Ratings

Hikes in this guide are scaled 1–10, 1 being the easiest, 10 being the most difficult. It is important to know that a 1 in this book may be an 8 in another guidebook. Mountain hikes are tough, there's no way around that. But once you've gotten a few under your boots, the relative scale of the difficulty will make sense.

Fit hikers will be able to complete all the hikes in this book—with good style! There are some long days and hard routes, but nothing that gets into elite or technical climbing. Beginning hikers can enjoy the lower difficulty hikes, especially summits like Peak 6.5, Uneva Peak, Loveland Pass west circuit, and Grays Peak.

As previously mentioned, the most difficult routes in this book are rated Class 3—but don't let that fool you. The hiking class designations are merely suggestions, and even Class 2 trails can be scary in bad conditions or if there's crazy exposure.

Here's a look at the (somewhat agreed upon) rating system used in Colorado:

- **Class 1:** Nontechnical, easy terrain. This is reserved mostly for simple trails or very low angle grassy slopes. Class 1 can still be steep but lacks any big fall risks.

- **Class 2:** This is your standard-issue hiking terrain: rocky trails, a few steep sections, the occasional easy scramble or big step. Fall potential is very low or nonexistent.

- **Class 2+:** A good designation for Class 2 with extended but safe scrambling or off-trail routes with rock outcrops. Scrambles are solid and always have bail-out options. This is the most advanced terrain that is safe to take dogs on.

- **Class 3:** Sustained, advanced scrambling with hands and feet with low fall potential but medium to high consequences from a fall. Rock is normally solid and helmets may be advised. Some Class 3 is on very solid rock with big exposure.

- **Class 4:** Class 4 is essentially low-level rock climbing, and ropes are sometimes used on Class 4 terrain. In general, the rock is solid, risk of fall is low, but consequences are high—fatalities have happened when climbers underestimate Class 4 routes. This book doesn't cover any Class 4 routes, though there may be moves on certain routes that could be somewhere between Class 3 and 4. Experienced climbers and those used to exposure generally are confident on Class 4.

- **Class 5:** Technical climbing, where rock climbing shoes, mountaineering boots, ropes, and harnesses are usually used. Not covered in this guide.

All ego aside, this book rates routes a bit conservatively. When there are explicitly dangerous Class 3 moves, they will be mentioned. For many of us, those are the most exciting parts of a climb! Ultimately, it is up to hikers to use their best judgment and know their abilities when tackling mountain hikes.

Optional Routes

Along with the standard routes, each chapter has a collection of optional routes. Many of these point-to-points make for fun, extended adventures that cover a lot of ground. Additionally, some of the routes that *didn't* make it into the book appear in trip write-ups online (mountainouswords.com/I70-hikes) to describe why they weren't up to par. There are many more options than presented in the book (such as hiking from "Golden Bear Peak" from the Loveland Tunnel West Trailhead all the way to Guenella Pass!), but with all the optional entries, there are more than 100 possible routes within these pages to keep the most avid hiker busy for a long time!

When deciding the radius of hikes, a max distance of 10 miles off I-70 is the sweet spot. By increasing that range by a mere 2 miles, dozens of new trailheads become available—and there are only so many pages available! However, some of the hikes that are very close still make it into this guide, albeit in truncated form. Many of these hikes have detailed GPS files available for free at the official book site: mountainouswords.com/I70-hikes. You're bound to be drawn to some of the nearby peaks you see from the summits of the "official" mountains, so adding them online gives added value to his book!

There are also a few places worth visiting while you'll be in the mountains, such as old mines, plane wrecks, and eerie cemeteries.

It's a three-dog day along the 7:30 Mine Trail (see page 41).

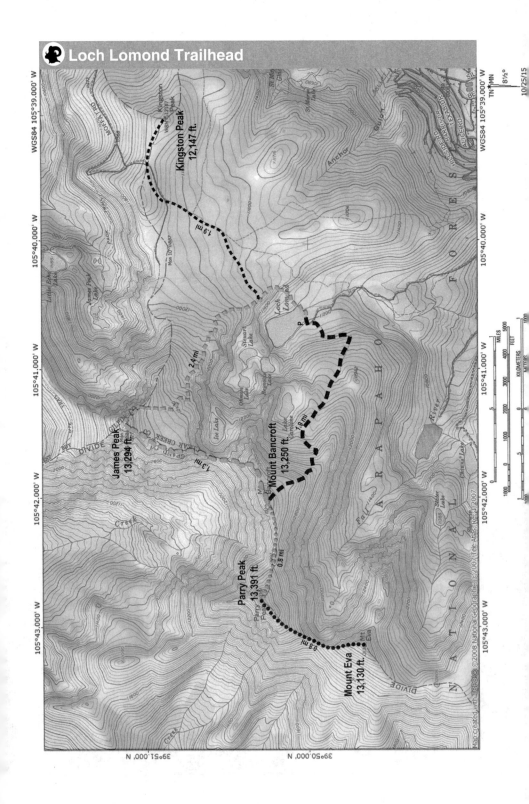

I. Loch Lomond Trailhead (11,215')

Loch Lomond's access road has a mellow grade offset by thousands of suspension-shaking rocks. SUVs and tough SUCs can make the trailhead without too much trouble; strong tires will boost your confidence. From the loch, enjoyable rolling slopes pass by several lovely lakes before topping off at 13,250-foot Mount Bancroft. James Peak and Parry Peak are also good options from this area.

PEAKS

- Mount Bancroft: 13,250'
- James Peak: 13,294'
- Parry Peak: 13,391'
- Mount Eva: 13,130'
- Kingston Peak: 12,147'

Wilderness Area and Range

James Peak Wilderness, Front Range

Trailhead Distance from I-70

11.6 miles

Driving Directions

From either eastbound or westbound I-70, take Exit 238 toward Fall River Road. Follow the paved, twisting Fall River Road a little over 7.5 miles and take a left onto Alice Road (initially paved). Drive up a steep hill just after the road turns to dirt, passing through the homes in the tiny town of Alice. Around mile 8.2, bear right onto Steuart Road and follow it 3.4 miles to the large parking area. This four-wheel drive isn't steep, but it is littered with rocks, some the size of volleyballs, all the way up—it's a bouncy ride. Stay on the main road. The parking area at the loch is large, and there are true four-wheel-drive roads that split west and east from here. Park here unless you have a modified four-wheel drive ready to roll.

Vehicle Recommendations

SUVs and tough, higher-clearance SUCs (Honda CR-Vs and Elements, Toyota RAV4s) can make it up this road. Rocks, rocks, and more rocks will be a test of strong tires and sturdy suspension, but there are never any technical rock outcrops nor is it steep—just bumpy.

Fees/Camping

There are no fees to park, hike, or camp. Camping is allowed in Arapaho National Forest, and there are a few primitive sites at the trailhead, but no restrooms. Please use leave-no-trace guidelines when camping.

Dog Regulations

Dogs are allowed on leash in the James Peak Wilderness.

Summary

Author's note: I made an exception to the "10-mile max distance" rule for this trailhead because I find it to be a fantastic hiking area, and it also provides a solid route to James Peak that avoids the private, paid parking used to access the St. Mary's Glacier area.

Loch Lomond is the sister area to Fall River Reservoir, though it's a little grittier and sees slightly more traffic. Loch Lomond isn't without charm however, thanks to the waterfalls that roll over the headwall into the lake. The backdrop of Mount Bancroft's popular Class 5 east ridge to the immediate north is quite impressive as well. The Class 2 route up to Mount Bancroft really shines once it departs a four-wheel-drive road past the parking lot and rises up above a collection of beautiful lakes. The off-trail terrain is easy to navigate, and Bancroft's summit, while well earned, is less taxing than other trail-free peaks. The walk over to Parry Peak is 0.8 mile and worth every step (Parry is the high point of the James Peak Wilderness).

The other primary route from Loch Lomond is a loop of James Peak and Mount Bancroft. This is an alternate to James Peak's standard route via St. Mary's Glacier and avoids the private, paid parking area at the previously free St. Mary's Glacier access off the paved Fall River Road.

Primary Routes

1. ✪ South Slopes of Mount Bancroft (13,250') to Parry Peak (13,391')

Round-Trip Distance	5.3 miles
Class	2
Difficulty	4/10
Hiking Time	5–6 hours
Total Elevation Gain	2,760'
Terrain	Hike a brief four-wheel-drive road to open, rolling terrain with excellent footing and modest grades. There are no official trails after the four-wheel-drive road ends, but navigation is straightforward.
Best Time to Climb	June–September

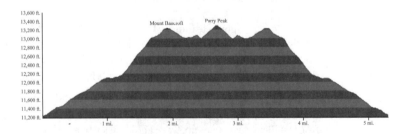

Overview   For those who love pure hiking, it's tough to beat this route for sheer scenery, welcoming terrain, and the chance to grab two lesser-visited thirteeners. It's also an excellent dog adventure. It's not a huge stretch to tack on Mount Eva (0.8 mile from Parry Peak) as an out-and-back. Hikers are somewhat rare here—most of the visitors to this area are four-wheel-drive enthusiasts who come to enjoy the fishing and knock back a few cold ones.

Ridge walking between Mount Bancroft and Parry Peak

Mile/Route **0.0** From the parking area, head south (away from Loch Lomond) and hike along the steep four-wheel-drive road. This initial push is a good warm-up and won't last long.

0.3 The four-wheel-drive road will switchback west and head up toward Bancroft's broad south slopes. Stay on it for now.

0.6 It's possible to gain the ridge here if you stick to the four-wheel-drive road up to a saddle, though the rocky part of the lower ridge is somewhat annoying to walk. Leave the four-wheel-drive road before ascending to the saddle, opting for the better route in the basin. There are faint trails in the basin, along with a trail north to Lake Caroline (a side trip of about 0.2 mile each way from the basin). Navigation will be easy despite no formal trail, as the south slopes will be on your left.

1.2 After walking northwest in the open basin, you'll approach the easiest slope to gain the south ridge at around 12,120 feet. It's about 400 vertical feet to get on the "ridge" (more of a rounded slope) that leads to Bancroft's summit.

1.4 Gain the ridge and carry on northwest to the top.

1.9 The summit! Depending on how much wandering you did in the basin, you will top out on Bancroft between 1.8 and 2.0 miles. Turn around now for a quick half-day outing (sometimes that's all we have time for). To continue to Parry, it's 0.8 mile along an easy ridge connecting the two.

2.7 After dipping down to 12,980 feet in the Bancroft–Parry saddle, a spirited push brings you to Parry's summit. All told at this point, 2,400 feet of elevation gain has occurred. You'll tack on another 300 on the return up and over Bancroft. Or continue to Eva, 0.8 mile from Parry. Going to Eva as an out-and-back is 7.1 miles with a burly 3,500+ feet of total elevation gain.

5.3 Return the way you came, over Bancroft. It can save a little time if you stay on the south slope ridgeline on the descent, connecting with the four-wheel-drive road in the low saddle at 11,900 feet. Finish mileage may vary depending on the off-trail path you choose, but expect between 5.3 and 5.5 miles round-trip.

2. James Peak (13,294')–Mount Bancroft (13,250') Loop

Round-Trip Distance	5.6 miles
Class	2
Difficulty	6/10
Hiking Time	5–7 hours
Total Elevation Gain	3,000'
Terrain	Well-traveled trails up to James Peak, then ridge walk over to Mount Bancroft and east, off-trail slopes to finish the loop.
Best Time to Climb	June–September

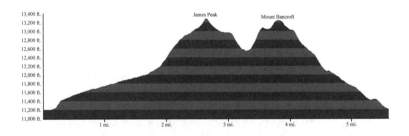

Overview Getting up to James Peak is straightforward—there is a trail directly from Loch Lomond all the way up. Despite the low mileage, this is a tough day due to the elevation gain. If you're up for more though, you can add on Kingston Peak (likely before summiting James) though James–Bancroft is more than enough for most people. Even an out-and-back up James Peak alone is a fine day.

The tastefully named James Peak is a tribute to Edwin James, a botanist from Vermont who climbed in Colorado in the mid-1800s. Besides claiming the first (white man) summit of James Peak, he also was the first (white man) to climb Pike's Peak (which was known as James Peak for a time).

Mile/Route **0.0** Follow the dam path along the southeast shore of Loch Lomond. A hiking trail will appear at the end of the wide path, heading north and

A quick dip in Lake Caroline with the famous rappel notch on
Mount Bancroft's East Ridge Route in the background

then west up James Peak's east slopes. The trail gets more pronounced the
higher it goes.

1.2 At this point, you'll be on the flats preceding the climb up to James
at 12,200 feet. If you want to add in Kingston Peak, now's the time to do
it. It's 1.2 miles to Kingston, but the way there is virtually flat. Toward
the end, there are 235 feet of elevation gain. It adds 2.4 miles to the day if
you choose this option. If not (which is the normal thing to do), carry on
along the trail to James Peak.

1.5 The standard route up James Peak merges with the Loch Lomond
route and continues to the top.

2.4 The summit of James Peak. Head south along the James–Bancroft
ridge, hitting the saddle (12,480') at mile 3.1. There are no trails, but the
traverse is straightforward. If the ridge feels exposed, the slopes on the
east side are less steep.

3.7 The summit of Bancroft. To complete the loop, follow Bancroft's
south slopes into the Lake Caroline Basin, then onward along the four-
wheel-drive road to Loch Lomond.

5.6 Finish

Notes Adding in Parry Peak adds 1.6 miles to the day but is a nice option if you're
still feeling strong when you reach Bancroft. Make certain you don't accidentally wander onto Bancroft's Class 5 east ridge on the descent.

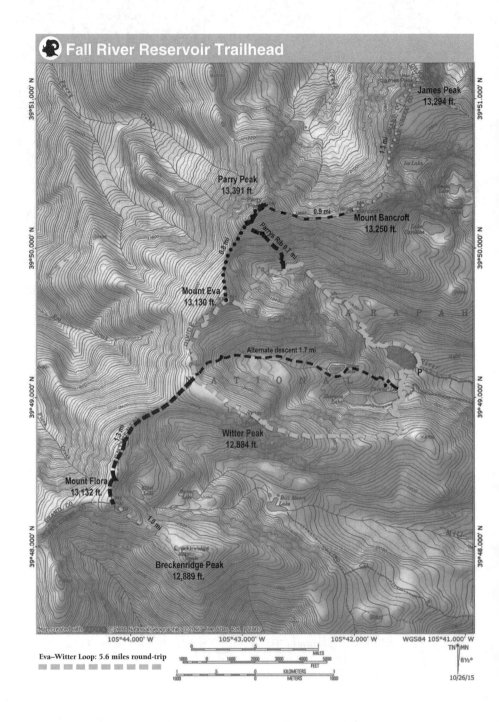

James Peak
13,294 ft.

Parry Peak
13,391 ft.

0.9 mi

Mount Bancroft
13,250 ft.

Parry's Rib 0.7 mi

Mount Eva
13,130 ft.

Alternate descent 1.7 mi

Witter Peak
12,884 ft.

Mount Flora
13,132 ft.

1.0 mi

Breckenridge Peak
12,889 ft.

Eva–Witter Loop: 5.6 miles round-trip

WGS84 105°41.000' W
TN MN
8½°
10/26/15

II. Fall River Reservoir Trailhead (10,750')

It's a bumpy ride to Fall River Reservoir but worth every jolt. Hike around the calm, cool waters of the reservoir, and then follow a cascade of wildflower-festooned waterfalls to one of the best-kept alpine secrets in the Front Range: the Fall River Basin. This wide-open alpine meadow is pure Colorado beauty. Several excellent summits await, with potential loops north or south. Don't miss the ruins of an old communication tower near the summit of Mount Eva.

PEAKS

- Parry Peak: 13,391'
- Mount Bancroft: 13,250'
- Mount Eva: 13,130'
- James Peak: 13,294'

- Witter Peak: 12,884'
- Breckenridge Peak: 12,889'
- Mount Flora: 13,132'

Wilderness Area and Range

James Peak Wilderness, Front Range

Trailhead Distance from I-70

9.6 miles

Driving Directions

From either eastbound or westbound I-70, take Exit 238 toward Fall River Road and reset your trip odometer. Head north on the paved Fall River Road. There are two wicked sharp switchbacks on this road; the first is at 4.5 miles. At the second switchback in 6.6 miles, turn left off the road, then take a quick right onto Rainbow Road (dirt). From here, it is 3.0 miles to Fall River Reservoir parking.

The dirt road is rocky but is fine for SUVs with four-wheel drive or all-wheel drive. Sport utility cars (SUCs) with high clearance (Honda CR-V/Toyota RAV4) can make the trailhead if carefully driven. The first 2 miles are relatively easy four-wheel-drive terrain. Be sure to stay on the wide, well-traveled main road—there are dozens of side roads that branch off along the way. At mile 6.7, you'll arrive at a fork in the road. Stay right for Fall River Reservoir. The left branch goes to Chinns Lake parking. The last 0.8 mile is the roughest, so if you have a marginal off-road vehicle, consider parking here. It's 0.9 mile to Chinns Lake from this junction (worth knowing if you have to park here and want to loop Mount Eva and Witter Peak). However, if you made it this far, the last section to the trailhead is just a touch steeper and rockier than what you've already driven. Park on the right, flatter side or unleash your inner four-wheel-drive beast and hammer up the steep, short hill on the left to the jeep parking (about 100 feet farther than the flat parking).

Vehicle Recommendations

SUVs and tough SUCs will be able to make it to Fall River Reservoir, though all-wheel drive and lower-clearance vehicles should take it easy on the bouncy rocks.

Fees/Camping   There are no fees to park, hike, or camp. Camping is allowed in Arapaho National Forest, and there are a few primitive sites at the trailhead, but no restrooms. Please use leave-no-trace guidelines when camping.

Dog Regulations   Dogs are allowed on leash in the James Peak Wilderness.

Summary   Peak baggers rejoice; there's a lot to get done out of this trailhead. Even in the height of summer, foot traffic to these mountains is very low (though there's likely to be a lot of people fishing or just hanging out at the reservoir). From the trailhead, the direct northeast ridge of Mount Eva (Class 3–4) makes quite an impression. This guide uses the traditional hiking route that skirts to the north and avoids this ridge. There aren't any formal trails, but getting around the reservoir and into the basin above requires easy, off-trail navigation—just follow the waterfalls.

A recurring theme in this guide is the sheer number of combinations and route options available from each trailhead, and this one is no exception. Snag several peaks, or just go out and back. A tour north gains the mountain ridges via Parry's surprisingly fun southeast rib. From there, Mount Bancroft and James Peak are a fun northern loop, while Parry–Eva to the south is just as good. For a direct line up Eva, stay in the basin and hit a steep but sturdy grass slope to Eva's southeast ridge saddle. From there, a fun Class 2+ scramble tops out on an extremely scenic summit. An easy 1.2-mile jaunt from Eva goes to the flat summit of Witter Peak, an unassuming summit with dramatic cliffs off its south face. A fun Class 2 scramble down Witter's East Ridge closes a high-quality loop to Chinns Lake. A brief flood-ravaged but passable drainage connects Chinns Lake with Fall River Reservoir.

Parry Peak, the high point in the James Peak Wilderness, is named for Dr. Charles Parry, a botanist and surveyor who was the first white man to climb and chart nearby Grays Peak in 1861. Mount Eva is named after his wife, though since she shared his last name, perhaps she could claim to have both peaks named in her honor?

Primary Routes

3. ✪ Northeast Ridge Slopes of Mount Eva (13,130') to Witter Peak (12,884')

Round-Trip Distance	5.6 miles
Class	2+
Difficulty	6/10
Hiking Time	5–6 hours
Total Elevation Gain	2,730'
Terrain	Off-trail with steep grassy slopes with good footing. Easy scramble down Witter Peak.
Best Time to Climb	June–September

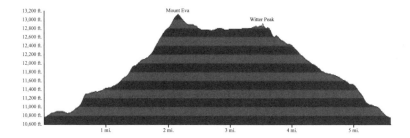

Overview   You could not bag a single peak in this circuit and still leave satisfied. The reservoir's mesmerizing, inky waters flow from a collection of small waterfalls and streams originating in the spacious alpine basin above. Snow tends to stick around all year, especially at the foot of the Parry–Eva saddle. This tour descends via Witter Peak's east ridge and has quite a surprise at the conclusion: following a flood-damaged drainage back to the trailhead!

Mile/Route   0.0   From the parking area, head north along the south shore of the reservoir. A broad, brief dirt road devolves into a climber's trail that makes a half circle to the west side of the reservoir. Morning sunlight often makes the water sparkle as if there were diamonds floating on the surface.
0.3   Leave the makeshift trail and follow even more makeshift trails up and west into the basin. You'll see Eva's imposing Class 3–4 ridge on your

Slater Lake (left) and Chinns Lake (right)

left; you won't be going up it just yet. There are some steep but sturdy scrambles to gain the basin. Staying close to the waterfalls on the right offers scenic access. Eventually, the trails fizzle out at the eastern forest of the basin proper (a great potential place for pitching a tent).

0.6 The grandiose basin will unfold before you. Go west young man, or woman, or possibly dog! Parry Peak will loom just off to your right and the Parry-Eva saddle will be in front of you. It looks mighty steep from here.

1.6 Eva's east ridge saddle comes into view to the southwest. It's a broad, steep grassy slope, but the footing is excellent (assuming there is no snow). If you've ever wondered what an 800-foot vertical wall of grass looks like . . . this is it. Chug along 0.4 mile from 12,000 feet to the saddle at 12,800 feet.

2.0 Phew! From the saddle, the west slopes to Eva's summit present about 300 vertical feet of really fun, solid, Class 2+ scrambling to the top. Staying right makes it a little easier, while the center has a bit more challenge.

2.2 The summit of Eva—hard to believe it's only 2.2 miles; it may feel longer. Just off the south of the summit are the ruins of an old communications tower that was fated to be removed in 2002. Apparently, it has some staying power. Time to head to Witter Peak, 1.6 miles away on gentle, easygoing slopes.

2.8 The Eva–Witter saddle. This is a possible return route, as shown on the map. There are a few willows to mash through, but navigation to Slater Lake/Chinns Lake is straightforward—just go down and east, staying to the left side of the basin. A trail emerges around Slater Lake just past a large, handmade stone shelter.

3.6 Witter's summit. While it's flat on one side, the south side cliffs are dramatic. The east ridge down has one notch to downclimb (Class 2+). If you have dogs, you may want to keep them on leash around the steep cliffs and possibly avoid this notch returning via the Eva–Witter saddle (1.75-mile basin walk to Chinns Lake, with a few willow thickets to navigate). But to stay on the route, head down the east ridge of Witter, downclimbing the notch and aiming for Chinns Lake.

4.7 When you are lined up with Chinns Lake, find a good slope to descend. It's a bit loose in places, but keep looking east to find a nice way down. Follow the south shore of Chinns Lake around 5.2 miles in. Stay north on the road and look for a stone-lined drainage past the northeast corner of the lake. This drainage connects Chinns to Fall River Reservoir.

Stay to the left of the drainage in the shady woods. It may feel off route, but it's a short no-trail jaunt down in an open forest. Stay on the left side of the drainage, marveling at some of the deep ravines cut into the land from the 2013 floods.

5.4 Keep following the drainage north. Soon you will see Fall River Reservoir through the trees. Eventually, you'll come to a few backcountry camp spots and the road back to the parking lot.

5.6 Finish.

Notes This route can be done in reverse, but that entails a descent of Eva's south slopes—not to mention fighting up the four-wheel-drive road to park at Chinns Lake (or walking it from below).

4. Parrys Rib to Parry Peak (13,391')–
Mount Bancroft (13,250')–Mount Eva (13,130') Loop

Round-Trip Distance	6.4 miles
Class	2+
Difficulty	6/10
Hiking Time	5–6 hours
Total Elevation Gain	3,070'
Terrain	Parrys Rib is a fun, if steep, scramble. Good rock until the middle, where the slopes get a little loose and sandy. Some off-trail, easy-to-navigate forest terrain at the start.
Best Time to Climb	June–September

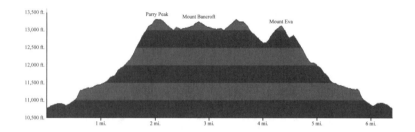

Overview Parrys Rib is a welcome route to the top of the highest peak in the James Peak Wilderness. It avoids a direct scree scramble up the Bancroft–Parry saddle (though there's still some loose, scrappy work near the summit). The walk over to Bancroft is a nice, relaxing saunter. You can return the way you came or link up several peaks. Looping down from Eva is popular (eschewing Bancroft is always an option as well).

Mile/Route 0.0 This hike follows the same route as Mount Eva for 1.6 miles. Pass the reservoir on its north shore, then head west over a series of low-angle waterfalls and gain the basin.

1.6 Split from the Mount Eva route at the base of the rib at 11,800 feet. There's some good Class 2+ scrambling to be had here, along with rock outcrops that offer more-challenging options. At 12,800 feet, a small shelf signals the end of the fun scrambling and the beginning of the loose, gravel-ridden slopes to the ridgeline.

2.1 Gain Parry's south ridge, just below the summit. The western side of these peaks along the Continental Divide is mellow and fun to traverse.

2.3 Parry's summit. There are lots of options from here. It's 0.9 mile to Bancroft, which is often done as an out-and-back, going back down Parrys Rib (though another fun option is to leave a second car at Loch Lomond and do a point-to-point, possibly tacking on James Peak).

6.4 Finish, if you've returned via Parrys Rib. Mount Eva is 0.8 mile from Parry; if you skip Bancroft and go directly to Mount Eva, then descend

Wide-open land in the basin above Fall River Reservoir

via the steep, grassy northeast slopes, the loop is about 5.4 miles round-trip. If you combine Parry, Bancroft, and Eva, it's a 7.3-mile loop—still a very manageable day for most hikers.

Additional Routes

Prepare for a recurring theme in this guide: lots of great options. This area is especially good for linking up peaks, since the terrain on the west side of the Continental Divide is mellow, accommodating, and quite scenic (the views from here are a nice preview of many other mountains in the book). Good, long days await strong and motivated hikers.

The Witter Slam: Witter, Eva, Parry, Bancroft, and James Peak Point-to-Point Ending at Loch Lomond

Class 2+ – 8.2 miles – 4,300' elevation gain

This requires one car parked at Loch Lomond and another at either Fall River Reservoir or Chinns Lake. The route can be truncated by starting at Fall River Reservoir and leaving out Witter Peak, but for a big, fun day (perfect for an autumn outing), start at Chinns Lake and reverse the Eva–Witter Loop. Traverse from Witter to James Peak along the Continental Divide, then descend James Peak's moderate east slopes, following trails south to Loch Lomond, where vehicle two will park.

Fall River Reservoir–Berthoud Pass Point-to-Point

Class 2+ – 8.2 miles – 3,780' elevation gain

Have a friend driving back home from Winter Park? Have him or her meet you at vehicle two at the summit of Berthoud Pass. This tour starts out the same as the Eva–Witter Loop from Fall River Reservoir and (most likely) skips Witter—unless you want to snag it for a nice bonus summit. Walking along the Continental Divide entails easy, off-trail terrain among fields of crimson grass and wildflowers. Mount Flora (13,132') is a scenic high point—an out-and-back east to Breckenridge Peak at 12,889 feet from Flora's summit will add another 1.6 miles to your day. It's a worthwhile visit if you have the energy and clear weather. Wrap up your adventure passing (or tagging) 12,493-foot Colorado Mines Peak and follow a broad dirt road to Berthoud Pass parking.

Notes   Breckenridge Peak from Mount Flora (1 mile each way) is an underrated tour; it's worth a look. Another group of trails can access this area, specifically Breckenridge Peak, Mount Flora, and Flora–Witter saddle ridge from Bill Moore Lake. The reason that area only gets a brief mention here is that the roads to Bill Moore Lake are legit four-wheel-drive out of the town of Empire. I've driven to Bill Moore a few times, and the road tends to be muddy, rocky—a jeeper's delight, but not great for SUVs and SUCs. If you love some off-roading, however, it's a nice place to visit.

Fall River Reservoir and Chinns Lake have good car-camping opportunities at their trailheads.

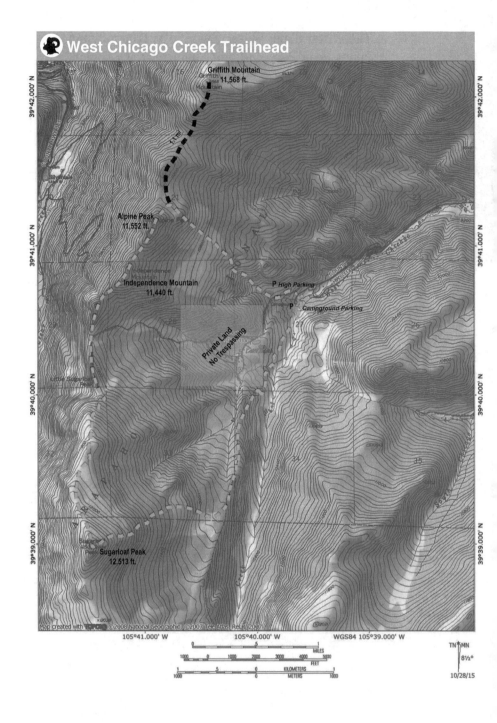

West Chicago Creek Trailhead

West Chicago Creek Trailhead (9,840')

If you like off-trail adventures to obscure peaks, this is your adventure. Private land makes this an interesting route. Unlike most hikes in this guide, the bulk of this adventure is done in the thick of treeline—make sure you are confident in your navigation skills before embarking on this one.

PEAKS
- Alpine Peak:11,552'
- Griffith Mountain: 11,568'
- Independence Mountain: 11,440'
- Sugarloaf Peak: 12,513'

Wilderness Area and Range
Arapaho National Forest, Mount Evans Wilderness, Front Range

Trailhead Distance from I-70
9.5 miles

Driving Directions
From I-70, take Exit 240 toward Mount Evans. Go south on CO 103 6.5 miles, then turn right onto Forest Service Road 188/West Chicago Creek Road. Stay on this well-maintained dirt road 3.0 miles to the campground area. Just before the campground area, across from some of the established sites, is a brief road that ramps uphill off to the right (north). Take this road up a few hundred feet to the higher parking area. This lot is also a more peaceful place to car camp.

Vehicle Recommendations
All vehicles can make it to the parking area, though the road can be snow covered into late spring and, of course, in winter.

Fees/Camping
No fees to hike. There are paid camping spots with restrooms for $16 and plenty of free, primitive camping in this area.

Dog Regulations
Leashed dogs are allowed in the campground. Arapaho National Forest allows dogs under voice control or on leash. Because this hike goes off-trail, through dense woods, and borders private land, do not bring your pup if you think he may run off. Once you enter Mount Evans Wilderness (near Sugarloaf Mountain), dogs must be on leash.

Summary
Late spring through early summer, West Chicago Creek's campground is a chaotic place. Screaming children by day, party animals rocking out into the night—let's say it's not exactly a good spot for peace and quiet. The one primary hiking trail out of this area (fittingly) goes to an old mining area known as Hells Hole. Unfortunately, the trail doesn't directly connect to any of the nearby mountains. Adding to the mix is a private community around Lake Edith that blocks the most direct access to the humble mountain range. Stumbling on this private property boundary reveals two facts about this community: They have a very large budget for NO TRESPASSING signs, and they are well armed.

However, this area has two redeeming qualities. The first is that, come autumn, the place quiets down a bit, especially when the paid campground closes in September. Secondly, the high point of this hike, Sugarloaf Peak, yields unique views of Georgetown, the I-70 corridor, and the swollen hills that top out at 14,264-foot Mount Evans. This is a good late-autumn or early-winter hike for those looking for something different. It's not terrible in the summer either because the bulk of the hiking is off-trail in the woods. You've been warned about the busy campground!

Primary Routes

5. Alpine Peak (11,552') to Sugarloaf Peak (12,513') Loop

Round-Trip Distance	7.2 miles
Class	2
Difficulty	5/10
Hiking Time	4–6 hours
Total Elevation Gain	3,100'
Terrain	Off-trail ascent and ridge walk through pine forest; return via well-established hiking trail.
Best Time to Climb	June–October

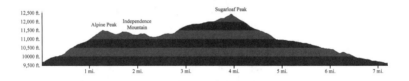

Overview If you're up to tackle this route, make sure you have some real experience navigating off-trail terrain that often has no line of sight. The bushwhacking itself is fairly tame, barring any patches of snow. The forest tends to be well spaced out, and the footing is good enough. Piercing treeline to ascend Sugarloaf is the big reward here. Be careful not to stumble into the private land around Lake Edith. In the woods, dozens of firm signs with many exclamation points say PRIVATE PROPERTY—NO TRESPASSING, just in case you forget.

Mile/Route 0.0 If you parked at the campground, hike back down the road (east) about 200 feet and take the right fork in the road up to the higher parking. A closed gate denoting the start of the private land appears along the road; please respect it. Your goal is to head straight west and bushwhack directly up through the woods to Alpine Peak, 1.2 miles away.

Several pseudotrails lead west through the evergreen groves. The good news is that this denser, darker forest quickly gives way to open fields of aspen. The higher you go, the more spaced out the flora becomes and the easier the navigation gets. Just aim for the high ridge.

1.2 At about this mileage, you'll arrive at the high ridge or quite possibly the summit of Alpine Peak itself. Alpine's summit has a large cairn and is open enough to afford good 360-degree views. If you really want to add on an obscure mountain, stay on the highest spine of the forested ridge and walk north 1.1 miles to Griffith Mountain. Otherwise, begin the ridge walk south toward Sugarloaf, which looks mighty big from here.

1.6 Cross the foresting minisummit known as Independence Mountain.

2.2 At a low point at the ridge, a few faded trails head down to the Lake Edith private community. The ridge is public national forest, so you're fine up high. The boundaries of the private land are far below. Continue to Sugarloaf Peak along steady, easy, Class 2 terrain.

3.9 Even though this summit is only 12,513 feet, you've climbed more than 3,100 vertical feet at this point.

   Note: While it's possible to range over to Grey Wolf Mountain, 4.2 miles away to the southeast, it's not a very enjoyable route. Descending off Grey Wolf requires good route-finding through acres of high willows to regain the

A look at the start of the challenging bushwhack to Sugarloaf from the Hells Hole Trail

southern terminus of the Hells Hole Trail. (If you're aiming to get Grey Wolf Mountain, Chicago Lakes Trail to the east is a much better option.)

Your next goal is to intercept the Hells Hole Trail, directly east of Sugarloaf. Descend 1.1 miles, starting with grassy/rocky slopes, then reentering the woods. Hells Hole Trail is well worn, but be wary when there is snow; it could be tough to locate.

5.0 Rejoin the Hells Hole Trail. Again, make a point not to wander toward the Lake Edith community. Once you've gotten on this trail, the bulk of the hard stuff is done. Head north on the trail, likely encountering many hikers on the way back. It's 2.2 miles back to the campground and parking.

7.2 Finish.

Extra, Extra Credit

North of Griffith Mountain is Saxon Mountain, an 11,546-foot peak. It's a fun mountain bike or four-wheel-drive road . . . or if you want to get in miles and a good workout, it can be hiked. Take Exit 228 to Georgetown, then turn east onto 15th Street 0.2 mile, going past the visitor's center. At the end of this road, go left onto Main Street. In 0.4 mile, this becomes Saxon Mountain Road, which is drivable for a while before becoming a true four-wheel-drive road. It's 8.0 miles one way, with 2,500 vertical feet of elevation gain, and there are 30 switchbacks to deal with.

So as a hike . . . not that great, at least if you're gunning for the top. It is a decent little hike to get in a few miles and turn back, however. And it's a fun mountain bike challenge in the summer.

IV. Empire–Republican Mountain Trailhead (9,570') and Bard Creek Trailhead (10,150')

Republican Mountain is best accessed by the Democrat and Republican Mountain four-wheel-drive road (the best way to hike the peaks in this section). The Bard Creek Trail is slowly fading from existence but provides an interesting alternative to reach these peaks—which are some of the most overlooked in the Front Range. Fans of fourteeners can brag about hiking Columbia (not that Columbia), Democrat (not that Democrat), and Sherman (not that Sherman) in the same day.

Note: *The Silver Plume–based 7:30 Mine Trail accesses these same peaks from the south and is a much easier trailhead for passenger cars (and drivers who don't want to beat up their SUVs). The caveat is that the route from Silver Plume requires a mile of relatively easy off-trail navigation. See page 38 for details.*

PEAKS

- Republican Mountain: 12,386'
- Sherman Mountain: 12,287'
- Silver Plume Mountain: 12,477'
- Bard Peak: 13,641'
- Robeson Peak: 13,141'
- Engelmann Peak: 13,362'
- Mount Parnassus: 13,574' (see page 40)

Wilderness Area and Range

Arapaho National Forest, Front Range

Trailhead Distance from I-70

Republican Mountain (lower parking): 4.8 miles
Bard Creek: 6.9 miles

Driving Directions

For both trailheads: Take Exit 232 to US 40 toward Empire. Follow 2.0 miles into the center of town, then take a left south onto South Main Street, also known as County Road 252 (if you have eagle eyes, you can see the words BARD CREEK in supertiny font on the South Main Street sign). South Main turns into Bard Creek Road. At 3.1 miles, pass a lake and small community on the right. From here, the road gets rougher. Lower-clearance cars should take it easy, and with careful driving, passenger cars can reach the well-signed turnoff four-wheel-drive road left to Republican and Democrat Mountains at 3.9 miles. Passenger cars would be wise to park here, if not sooner.

To Republican Mountain: The entire length of this road is 3.8 miles, but it's heinously rocky and quite steep in sections. Four-wheel drives and high-clearance SUVs with good tires can get up to the high-point parking (which is a mile from Republican's summit); however, there's a good SUV parking

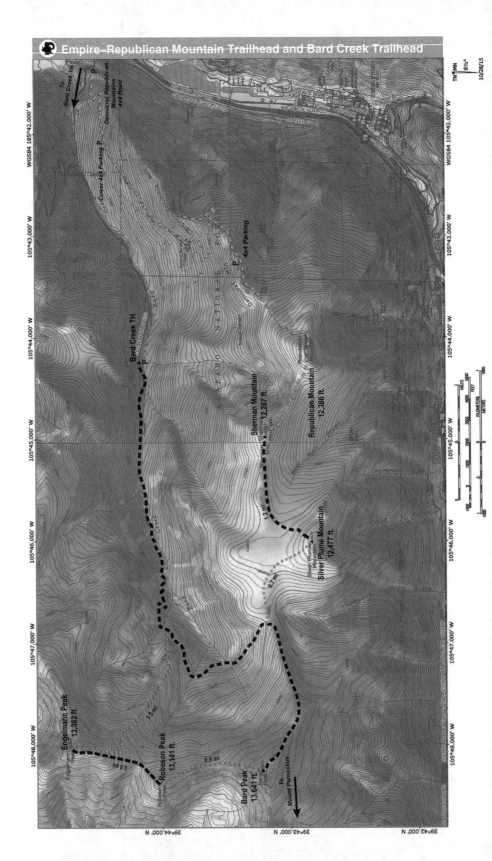

Empire–Republican Mountain Trailhead and Bard Creek Trailhead

area at 0.7 mile. This small pulloff to the right is good parking for SUVs. The rest of the road is rocky but never super exposed or technical—just steep and very, very rocky. At 2.1 miles up the road, stay left on the main road at 10,610 feet. Jeeps/four-wheel drives should park 3.8 miles up at 11,410 feet. This four-wheel-drive road does continue down and south . . . don't follow it!

To Bard Creek Trailhead: To reach the Bard Creek Trailhead, ignore the turnoff to the Democrat and Republican Mountains and stay straight onto Forest Service Road 777.1. It's 2.2 miles from the turnoff to the trailhead along a four-wheel-drive road. Stay on the main road, avoiding several turnoffs along the way. SUCs can get down this road about 1.4 miles, but the last 0.8 mile is very rocky. High-clearance four-wheel drives can fight it out up the rocky road to the parking area. Bard Creek Trail starts here.

Vehicle Recommendations	Those with passenger cars may want to get these peaks via the 7:30 Mine Trail in Silver Plume (see page 38). The four-wheel-drive roads are nice hikes with good shade, so it's actually a pleasant walk.
Fees/Camping	There are no fees to hike or camp in this area of Arapaho National Forest.
Dog Regulations	Dogs are allowed under voice control or on leash.
Summary	Republican Mountain is an unexpected treat in a seldom-visited area. Besides the fantastic views, both of these trailheads can be used as a launching pad for day hikes and big traverses, including a point-to-point to Watrous Gulch (with additional peaks Engelmann Peak, Robeson Peak, and Woods Mountain in striking range). On the map, Democrat Mountain and Columbia Mountain are mere subpeaks on the shoulder of Republican Mountain—it makes one wonder what political conspiracies contributed to these names. Hiking along the four-wheel-drive roads is actually quite pleasant, thanks to the shade from bristlecone pines. The Bard Creek Trail has been neglected and thus has a habit of disappearing—however, if you're in it for the summits, you'll want to split from this 11.4-mile trail and hike the ridges (Bard Creek Trail starts in Empire and ends in Watrous Gulch). The hiking here is easy, though there are no formal trails to any of the peaks past the roads. A great doggy destination!

Primary Routes

6. Republican Mountain (12,386') and Sherman Mountain (12,287')

Round-Trip Distance	From start at Democrat and Republican four-wheel-drive road: 11.0 miles; from SUV parking at 9,570': 9.5 miles; from high four-wheel-drive parking: 3.4 miles
Class	1
Difficulty	3/10
Hiking Time	Varies depending on starting point; 4–7 hours

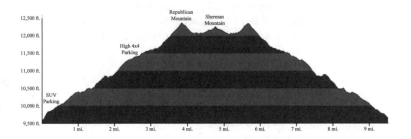

Total Elevation Gain	3,677' from start of road at 8,900'
Terrain	Four-wheel-drive road with easy-to-navigate, low-angle, off-trail slopes to the peaks along grassy earth
Best Time to Climb	Late May–October

Overview Whether you're walking the road or starting up high, the Republican Mountain area is worth a visit. There are a lot of mining ruins along the way, most of them simple mounds of earth and a few stray timbers. The peak itself has an enjoyable walk-up, and continuing west opens up a spectacular alpine park above treeline. It's an easy walk down to the nearly flat summit of Sherman Mountain. Those aiming for a bigger day can tack on the quirky summit of Silver Plume Mountain or go big and bag 13,641-foot Bard Peak.

Mile/Route 0.0 The start of Democrat and Republican four-wheel-drive road.

0.7 At 9,570 feet, a nice mid-mountain parking area appears on the right for SUVs after a particularly rocky, steep section of road. The road doesn't get much more difficult or steeper than it already has been . . . but it's slow going. Not a bad place to start your adventure.

2.1 The old mining ruins of Rodgers Shaft offer a nice viewpoint. Stay left on the main road, switchbacking east for a short distance, then south before resuming west.

3.8 At 11,481 feet, treeline becomes sparse and the large dome of Republican Mountain looms to the west. You have arrived at Democrat Mountain and the high four-wheel-drive parking. Park (or continue hiking) and navigate through an open field of shrubs and a few mining ruins above treeline and head straight on to Republican Mountain. There are no official trails, but there are a few faint hiker's paths. Near the summit, stay slightly south and bypass a few "rock crowns" on the shoulder of Republican before topping out.

4.6 The rocky, relaxing summit of Republican Mountain. To continue to Sherman, head northwest on the broad connecting ridge. Sherman looks like a mere bump from here but is a bit more mountainous upon closer inspection.

5.5 Sherman's quaint summit. From this vantage, the top of Republican Mountain wears a rocky crown. Return the way you came, taking time to peek south at the traffic rushing on I-70.

11.0 Finish at the bottom of the four-wheel-drive road.

photographed by Paul Lenhart

The last push to the summit of Republican Mountain

Notes Silver Plume Mountain is 1.2 miles one way from Sherman along open
      alpine tundra. It's a fun summit to visit thanks to the 10-foot-tall summit
      boulder that requires bouldering moves to top out (there are rock steps
      and a wood "step" that help). Bard Peak is a stiffer task: 3.2 miles one way
      from Silver Plume with 1,940 feet of elevation gain. If starting from the
      high parking, it's about 12 miles round-trip (depending on how directly
      you hike on the tundra) with 3,700 feet of elevation gain—a good day for
      strong hikers that grabs four peaks.

7. Bard Peak (13,641') via Bard Creek Trail

Round-Trip Distance	11 miles
Class	2
Difficulty	6/10
Hiking Time	6.5–8.5 hours
Total Elevation Gain	3,810'
Terrain	Old, forested trail climbs above treeline, where navigation on alpine tundra and high ridges gets easier. Rocky but stable foot leads all the way up to Bard Peak.
Best Time to Climb	June–September

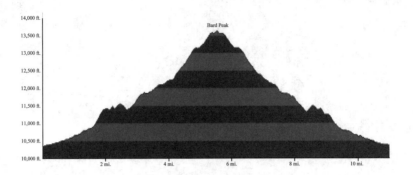

Overview   Because of its somewhat isolated location, there's no easy way up Bard Peak. It can be accessed a number of ways, and the Bard Creek Trail is the closest thing it has to a standard route. Follow the neglected Bard Creek Trail over downed trees until it dissolves above treeline. Luckily, at this point ridges are easy to locate and follow, but a GPS is helpful for finding your way back down (especially if there is snow cover). When in doubt, follow Bard Creek. Navigation can be difficult at times.

Author's note: Navigating to Bard Peak is easiest from Herman Gulch (see page 62). The route up from the 7:30 Mine Trail (see page 41) is also a good option.

Mile/Route   **0.0**   Starting at the end of the four-wheel-drive road, head west on the Bard Creek Trail. The trail is in rough shape but sees enough traffic to remain visible. Stay on it as it switchbacks along Bard Creek toward treeline.

2.5   After following Bard Creek since the start of the trail, head south away from the creek (whose headwaters begin from the slopes of Engelmann Peak). The trail has the habit of fading away and reappearing. Once you break treeline, aim for the saddle between Silver Plume Mountain and Bard Peak.

4.1   At 12,015 feet, the terrain goes flat. Line up the curving, east ridge of Bard Peak and get rolling—it's 1,580 vertical feet and 1.4 miles to the top.

5.5   13,641 feet and you can go no higher. Bard Peak is the highest member of this group of mountains and the views are fittingly fantastic. Return back the way you came.

11.0   Finish back at the Bard Creek Trailhead.

Notes   Silver Plume Mountain is 0.7 mile from the flat saddle at the foot of Bard Peak's east ridge. It's a tougher add-on than it might seem on a map, with 426 feet of elevation gain and an additional 1.4 miles round-trip to your total day. Still, if you're up here it's a good one to grab.

Of course, it's completely reasonable to skip Bard Peak altogether and use the Bard Peak Trailhead to access Silver Plume, Sherman, and Republican.

Bard Peak, seen from Silver Plume Mountain

From the summit of Bard Peak, it's a mostly downhill walk 0.9 mile to 13,141-foot Robeson Peak. Engelmann Peak (13,362') is 0.9 mile from Robeson Peak (this route is 710 vertical feet and 1.8 miles away from Bard Peak). The quickest way back is via Engelmann's southeast ridge (see below).

Engelmann Peak Southeast Ridge via Bard Creek Trailhead

Class 2+ – 8.4 miles round-trip – 3,325' elevation gain

This challenging route is a fun option for strong hikers with good route-finding skills. Experience with navigation is a must. Follow the Bard Creek Trail (or what there is of it) about 2.6 miles. Adjacent to a clear-cut patch of trees, go off-trail at 11,660 feet and gain Engelmann's long southeast ridge. It's 1.5 miles to the summit. From here, link up Robeson Peak and Bard Peak, or simply return the way you came.

Engelmann Peak is named in honor of botanist George Engelmann, whose other famous namesake is the Engelmann Spruce.

Republican Mountain to Herman Gulch Traverse

Class 2+ – 9.4 miles point-to-point – 3,800' elevation gain

An exceptional traverse (see map), this route can be hiked either way. The tricky part is leaving a vehicle at the high parking on Democrat Mountain . . . then retrieving that car later. Logistically, this route can also be done via the non-four-wheel-drive parking available at the 7:30 Mine Trail, but that option misses out on easily getting Republican and Sherman Mountains. Follow the ridges up Republican to Sherman, up Bard, over to Mount Parnassus. Descend via Mount Parnassus's west slopes, into Watrous Gulch, and follow the Watrous Gulch Trail to Herman Gulch, where your second vehicle awaits. Four big peaks with the option of tacking on Silver Plume Mountain and/or Woods Mountain for an utter monster of a day.

V.   Silver Plume–7:30 Mine Trailhead (9,175')

The 7:30 Mine Trail is one of the true hidden hiking gems off I-70. This well-maintained, Class 1 trail passes several impressive mine ruins, all the time offering excellent views of the I-70 corridor below. The trail ends at the Griffin Monument at Brown Gulch. Intrepid peak baggers must head off-trail into the woods to get above treeline. Silver Plume Mountain is the marquee peak, featuring a nifty summit block scramble.

PEAKS

- Silver Plume Mountain: 12,477'
- Bard Peak: 13,641'
- Robeson Peak: 13,141'
- Engelmann Peak: 13,362'
- Mount Parnassus: 13,574'
- Republican Mountain: 12,386'
- Sherman Mountain: 12,287'

Wilderness Area and Range

Arapaho National Forest, Front Range

Trailhead Distance from I-70

0.3 mile

Driving Directions

Take Exit 226 to Silver Plume. At the end of the westbound exit, turn right onto a dirt road (Woodward Street). Eastbound, turn left off the exit and go under the I-70 bridge to reach the same point. Go about 300 feet to the end of this road, then turn right onto Main Street (also dirt). In about 400 feet, turn left onto Silver Street and follow this dirt road up a hill 400 feet to the trailhead parking. Note that there's only room for about three or four vehicles at this unpolished trailhead. If parking is not available at the trailhead, the town of Silver Plume requests that you park on Main Street in town (only an extra 400 feet to walk to the trailhead).

Vehicle Recommendations

Any vehicle. Passenger cars should park on Main Street at the intersection Main and Silver.

Fees/Camping

There are no fees to camp or hike in this section of the Arapaho National Forest.

Dog Regulations

Dogs are allowed under voice control or leashed.

Summary

The first section of this adventure, the 7:30 Mine Trail, is an excellent day hike in its own right (and a good one to visit if you're sick of being stuck in traffic). It's 1.8 miles long and tours a collection of closed mines, ending at the 7:30 Mine itself (so named because the work day started at 7:30 a.m., an hour later than a normal mining day at the time). At the western terminus of the trail, the impressive monument to former 7:30 Mine manager

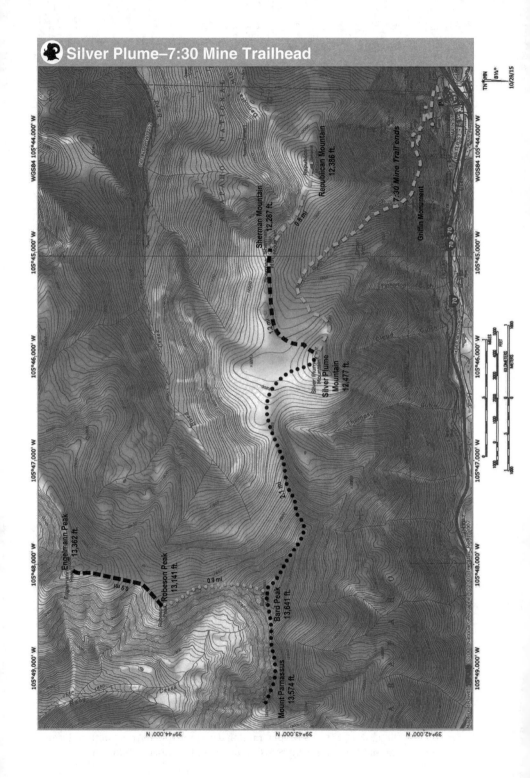

Silver Plume–7:30 Mine Trailhead

Engelmann Peak
13,362 ft.

Robeson Peak
13,141 ft.

Bard Peak
13,641 ft.

Mount Parnassus
13,574 ft.

0.9 mi

2.1 mi

Silver Plume
Mountain
12,477 ft.

Sherman Mountain
12,287 ft.

1.2 mi

Republican Mountain
12,386 ft.

0.8 mi

7:30 Mine Trail ends

Griffin Monument

TN MN
8½°
10/28/15

Clifford Griffin watches over the town (read more about his story and monument in the "Notes" section on the next page). Past the trail, bushwhack through the woods, where trails appear and disappear amid hidden mine ruins. Break treeline into an impressive alpine tundra and continue to Silver Plume Mountain's notorious summit block. Several optional summits are nearby, with Sherman and Republican Mountains being the easiest to reach.

Primary Routes

8. ✪ Silver Plume Mountain (12,477') via the 7:30 Mine Trail

Round-Trip Distance	8.0 miles
Class	2+
Difficulty	6.5/10
Hiking Time	5–7 hours
Total Elevation Gain	3,520'
Terrain	Easy, wide trail changes to off-trail wandering through the woods to reach treeline, then an easy walk up to the summit. Summit block requires a scramble.
Best Time to Climb	Mid-June–October

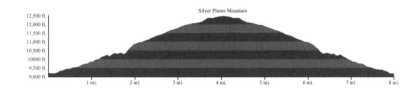

Silver Plume Mountain

Overview A personal favorite, this adventure starts off along a wide trail that passes impressive mining ruins. Views up the valley along the I-70 corridor are incredible. After a good warm up on the established trail, hop over Brown Gulch and go off-trail through about a mile of pine forests before breaching treeline. Past the woods, the wide-open tundra offers an easy walk-up to Silver Plume's summit block, where an interesting finishing scramble awaits.

Mile/Route **0.0** The trailhead parking area has some interesting mine ruins and a mini-sluice. The trail is well signed and begins uphill to the east. Off you go!
0.5 More big mine ruins along the second switchback. Continue switchbacking up the trail. Views along this stretch are already awe-inspiring, in the true sense of the word. What must these mines have been like in the 1880s?
0.9 The trail passes over Cherokee Creek and continues west.
1.1 More mining ruins at another switchback. Carry on east to the next switchback.
1.8 The end of the official trail at 10,400 feet. A heavily gated, closed mine is on the right side of the trail, while the Griffin monument can

be seen on a rocky, cliffed outcrop to the south. It's worth a look before heading on. A short access trail goes from the end of the 7:30 Mine Trail to Brown Gulch.

1.9 The Brown Gulch crossing is littered with rusted-out boilers from another age. In spring, this modest creek can run hard and fast—be extra careful when crossing, especially if you have included dogs in your hike. Getting swept downhill would not be pleasant. This is the best crossing spot most times of the year. Cross the creek and the real fun begins. If you have GPS, mark a waypoint here for your trip back.

Note: Curious why you don't stay on the right (east) side of the creek? Actually, you can. When scouting out this hike for the first time, I did just that. There are few interesting scrambles, then a few steep, sandy hills to claw up as you head up the gulch. Hidden in the woods are pockets of old mining ruins and artifacts. Eventually, you'll be stuck bushwhacking through some very dense thickets, and it's quite a bit of work to get to treeline. It's fun . . . if you happen like that style of off-trail travel. The west side of the creek is much easier to navigate through, as there are hints of old miners' trails and the trees are comfortably spaced out most of the way. But if you're looking for some added challenge . . . be my guest to try the east side!

2.5 From the creek crossing, head north into the woods, keeping the creek to your right. There are faint trails that come and go, but nothing solid to follow. That's fine; the navigation is relatively easy since the trees are spaced out. Stay above the creek, but not too high. Most of the way you can keep the Brown Gulch Creek in site. At 2.5 miles, the forest thins down to low shrubs and the open, grassy slopes below Silver Plume Mountain appear.

3.2 Around this mileage, arrive on the broad flats between Sherman Mountain and Silver Plume Mountain. Head left (west) up the slopes to Silver Plume's summit, which is humbled by the massive-looking hunk of rock that is Bard Peak to the west.

4.0 What a curious summit. The summit block is comprised of a stack of boulders, the highest one being about a 6-foot mantle to top out on. Taller folks will have no problem, but those who are 5-foot-10 and below may appreciate a boost. An improvised wooden step has been in place for the last few years and will likely still be there. Just south of the summit is an old mining pit—watch out for rusty nails.

Return the way you came. Navigation back to the crossing point isn't very difficult, but pay attention. Keep an eye out for Griffin's monument—it's a good beacon.

8.0 Finish.

Notes Griffin's monument isn't just a tribute—it's also a grave. The sorrowful story of its occupant gives life to the cold stone that stands vigil over the oblivious traffic below.

Born in 1847, Clifford Griffin came to Colorado from New York after his fiancée unexpectedly passed away. Local lore, archived in the George Rowe Museum in Silver Plume, says that Clifford's brother owned the 7:30 Mine and invited his heartbroken sibling to manage the operations. Clifford proved to be a uniquely qualified leader of his men, giving them reasonable work hours, safe mining conditions, clean housing,

Silver Plume's summit with Bard Peak beyond

and giving every family a goose at Christmas. In an age of backbreaking labor, Griffin showed compassion and dignity for his miners—mostly Italian immigrants—and was beloved in Silver Plume.

Yet, with no family of his own, Griffin looked at the wives and children of his men with bittersweet affection. Absent in his own life was the love and companionship many of his workers enjoyed. On nearly every summer night, he took his loneliness and his violin to the mine entrance 1,500 feet above town. There, he would sit on the rocky outcrop—where the monument now stands—and fill the evening with beautiful music. Locals anticipated the nightly serenades, which often continued long past midnight.

Then one summer, as the legend goes, after a particularly passionate song on the violin, the silence of the night air was shattered by the crisp, sickening crack of a single gunshot. When his men rushed up to check on Clifford, they found him dead with a self-inflicted wound through his heart. His final thoughts were written in a note, wherein he humbly asked to be laid to rest in a grave he had dug into the hard earth. His brother, stunned with grief, obliged and added the monument you see today in 1887. Clifford Griffin was 40 years old.

Options

Sherman Mountain is 1.2 miles one way from Silver Plume Mountain, while Republican Mountain is 0.8 mile from Sherman. These are nice add-ons because they only add 400 total vertical feet, and hikers can descend back into Brown Gulch directly off Sherman, so all told it will add about 2

Rusty boilers denote the end of the trail and the beginning of the bushwhacking. Cross the creek here.

miles total. Or you can ignore Silver Plume Mountain altogether and just hike up Sherman and Republican Mountains.

Strong hikers may consider linking up with Bard Peak. Bard Peak is 2.1 miles from Silver Plume Mountain's summit and 1,610 feet higher. To go even bigger, connect Robeson Peak 0.9 mile away and Engelmann Peak, which is 0.9 mile north of Robeson. That makes for a monster day as an out-and-back—12.5 miles with a quad-fizzling 7,600 feet of total elevation gain. If it's a big day ye seek, there's your route.

On a less extreme note, the 7:30 Mine Trailhead is a good starting option for the point-to-point mentioned in the previous chapter on page 38. Starting here, the traverse of 10.8 miles and 5,800 feet of elevation gain grabs Silver Plume Mountain, Bard Peak, and Mount Parnassus. Follow Watrous Gulch down to the Watrous Gulch Trail and Herman Gulch, where car number two is waiting.

Extra Credit

If the spooky vibe of mine ruins appeals to you, consider visiting the little-known Silver Plume Cemetery. The gothic tombs and graves from the 1880s offer a personal glimpse into the hard lives of the miners (mostly of Italian descent). The graveyard is bigger than it initially looks, taking up most of the hill it occupies. Don't miss the large and tasteful monument on the west side of the cemetery. It's a tribute to miners killed in an avalanche. Many other statues, some decaying and moss covered, adorn the grounds. The cemetery is still in use today, though there are very few modern graves. Despite the hardscrabble history its story tells, Silver Plume Cemetery is a shady, quiet, and peaceful place.

It's less than a mile from the 7:30 Mine Trailhead. To get there, return to the highway exit off Woodward Street. Rather than return to the highway, stay on Woodward Street, passing under I-70. Pass the eastbound off-ramp and the westbound on-ramp, as well the turnoff for the railroad station on your left. Stay on this main dirt road (Mountain Street) as it climbs uphill and bends right, passing a small road to the left. After it straightens out, take the next left (there may be an open iron gate to pass) and follow it to a large parking area a few hundred feet farther. The cemetery gates are to the north. Park here. Please respect the private residence to the south, not only since it would be rude to trespass but also because there's a good chance the place may be haunted.

The pseudotrail above treeline

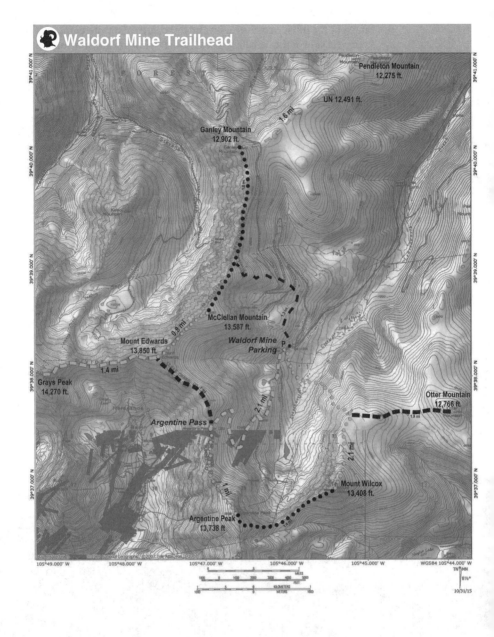

Pendleton Mountain
12,275 ft.

UN 12,491 ft.

1.6 mi

Ganley Mountain
12,902 ft.

McClellan Mountain
13,587 ft.

*Waldorf Mine
Parking*

Mount Edwards
13,850 ft.

0.8 mi

1.4 mi

Grays Peak
14,270 ft.

Otter Mountain
12,766 ft.

1.8 mi

2.1 mi

2.1 mi

Argentine Pass

1 mi

Mount Wilcox
13,408 ft.

Argentine Peak
13,738 ft.

105°49.000' W   105°48.000' W   105°47.000' W   105°46.000' W   105°45.000' W   WGS84 105°44.000' W

39°41.000' N

39°40.000' N

39°39.000' N

39°38.000' N

39°37.000' N

TN MN
8½°

10/31/15

VI.   Waldorf Mine Trailhead (11,630')

Mining history is rich at this four-wheel-drive accessible trailhead. Argentine Pass is the main draw here, offering a very nice hiking path up to Mount Edwards and Argentine Peak. There's also the opportunity to wander up to Ganley Mountain and McClellan Mountain, two peaks on the ridge that make up the eastern walls of nearby Stevens Gulch. Most SUVs and even high-clearance SUCs can make this trailhead, assuming they have enough muscle to get up a few steep, dirt roads at the start.

PEAKS

- Mount Edwards: 13,850'
- Argentine Peak: 13,738'
- Mount Wilcox: 13,408'
- Grays Peak: 14,270'
- McClellan Mountain: 13,587'
- Ganley Mountain: 12,902'
- UN 12,491: 12,491'
- Pendleton Mountain: 12,275'
- Otter Mountain: 12,766'

Wilderness Area and Range

Arapaho National Forest, Front Range

Trailhead Distance from I-70

9.8 miles

Driving Directions

Take Exit 228 to Georgetown, and then turn east onto 15th Street for about 250 feet. Turn right onto Argentine Street (there may be signs pointing to Guenella Pass Road). In 0.5 mile, turn left onto Sixth Street, and in 500 feet turn right onto Rose Street (which has signs for Guenella Pass). In 0.2 mile, turn left up Guenella Pass. This is a steep, paved road with tight switchbacks. At mile 3.5, take a tight switchback right, then left. An easy-to-miss dirt road heads up steeply into the woods. This is Leavenworth Creek Road, the four-wheel-drive access road to Waldorf Mine. There is a pair of parking areas here for those using mountain bikes or ATVs. Reset your odometer here.

All the difficult driving is within the first 1.1 miles of the road. Consult the special map on the next page for visual details. The first hill is steep, a little loose, but fairly easy Colorado four-wheel-drive terrain. Take the tight switchback to the right. The trick here is not taking any of the tempting side roads. Continue switchbacking up a series of steep hills. At 0.2 mile, there are some concrete buildings and a smooth road toward them (straight) and a steep, loose hill (right). Go right and up the hill. Congratulations, you've passed trap number one. (If you do accidentally take this road, it quickly ends, and you'll have to back out.)

At mile 0.9 is the big trap. Straight ahead is a smooth, inviting four-wheel-drive road (Forest Service Road 248.1B). To the right is a loose,

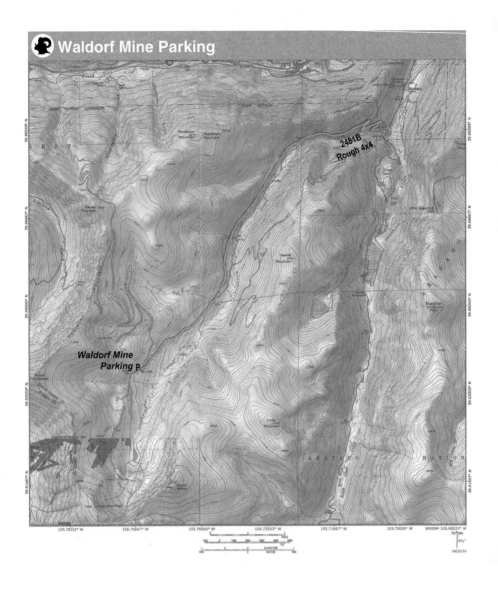

scrappy-looking dirt hill. Go right up the steep, loose hill. FR 248.1B starts off nice but then becomes a very rocky, at times technically tricky jeep road. (I made that mistake in my 4Runner and luckily bashed my way out.) It is a pretty fun drive for true four-wheel drives and jeeps, but stock SUVs will take a beating and SUCs will likely fall apart. So avoid it!

Once you get to the top of the steep, loose hill, turn left at mile 1.1. What a surprise! This wide shelf road could be a peaceful country road. The rest of this drive is easy. Stay on the wide, maintained dirt road 5.3 miles (avoiding any side roads) to arrive at the wide-open Waldorf Mine area. Jeeps and four-wheel drives can actually drive up to the top of

Argentine Pass, but it's a tough drive past the mine. Park at the mine and begin your adventure.

SUVs and high-clearance SUCs with a bit of muscle can make this trailhead. All the work on this four-wheel-drive road is at the start, where steep, loose hills with a few big rocks create the illusion of a tough drive to the trailhead. Good tires and good brakes are required. Once above the initial difficulties of the four-wheel-drive road (less than a mile) the route becomes a pleasant dirt road that leads directly up to the old mining area.

Fees/Camping There are no fees to camp or hike in this area of Arapaho National Forest.

Dog Regulations Dogs are allowed under voice control or on leash.

Summary After some interesting driving, a wealth of hiking awaits. The ridge walking in this area is fantastic. The terrain is never harder than Class 2+, and the openness of the area makes off-trail navigation easy. The mining ruins, especially to the north along McClellan Mountain and Ganley Mountain, are a bit of an eyesore for some. However, Mount Edwards, Argentine Peak, and Wilcox make for an excellent day hike that grabs three thirteeners. The Edwards to Grays traverse is a novel way to get one of the busier fourteeners (and sets up a possible point-to-point to Stevens Gulch or all the way to Loveland Pass).

Waldorf wasn't just a mine complex—it was an actual town in the late 1800s. At 11,666 feet, it once boasted America's highest post office. The building is still standing—it's the small hut under a utility pole near the wide-open parking area. More than $4 million of gold and silver were mined here from the Big Stevens Mine . . . maybe there's still some leftover nuggets to discover?

Primary Routes

9. ✪ Mount Edwards (13,850') to McClellan Mountain (13,587') Loop

Round-Trip Distance	6 miles
Class	2
Difficulty	5/10
Hiking Time	4–6 hours
Total Elevation Gain	2,400'
Terrain	Wide trails and four-wheel-drive roads that lead to easy-to-walk-on, solid, grassy slopes to the summits.
Best Time to Climb	June–October

Overview This loop is a great way to score one of Colorado's 100 highest peaks in Mount Edwards (either 82nd or 83rd highest, depending on the list you consult) and tack on a high thirteener in McClellan Mountain. The town

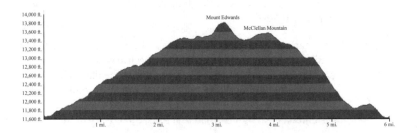

ruins of Waldorf are an interesting setting, with many old foundations, cables, and other mining debris strewn about (mining ceased in this area in the 1940s). Argentine Pass is a four-wheel-drive road but also quite a nice hike. Cascades of water often run down the ruts in the road. At the top of the pass at 13,207 feet, turn right (northwest) and hike up the mild slopes of Mount Edwards. Strong hikers can enjoy the Class 2+ walk/scramble over to Grays Peak as an added bonus.

Mile/Route   **0.0**   Argentine Pass is clearly visible from the Waldorf Mine parking area. Stay on the main road as it curves and switchbacks up the pass. Jeeps do sometimes take the road to the top, though they'll be moving slowly enough for you to see them coming.

2.1   Glorious views await at the top of the pass at 13,207 feet. To the west is Horseshoe Basin, another good trailhead accessed from the town of Montezuma. Turn off-trail and head northwest to the rounded summit of Mount Edwards.

2.3   Top out on Point 13,484 and carry on across the gentle slopes to the rocky crown of Mount Edwards.

3.1   The summit of Mount Edwards. Options abound. An out-and-back is one possibility, though the walk over to McClellan Mountain is a quicker route, plus it adds on another summit. Strong hikers may opt to grab Grays Peak, a very popular 14,000-foot mountain—but not from this route. You'll likely have the Class 2+ ridge to yourself for 1.4 miles until you top out on Grays.

This hike description covers the route to McClellan Mountain, 0.8 mile away from Edwards. Follow the rocky northeast slopes that connect the two. It's a nice walk, and you'll likely behold teeming activity in Stevens Gulch far below to the north.

3.9   The high point of McClellan Mountain signifies the summit. Amazingly, there was once a railroad up to McClellan Mountain from the north side via Stevens Gulch. Tourists paid to ride up a very steep grade, so consider yourself lucky—you got up here for free.

There's a matrix of four-wheel-drive roads and trails here. The Waldorf Mine (and your vehicle) will be visible below. Follow the roads, or hike directly down McClellan's northeast slopes, passing many old mining artifacts along the way. If you're going to add on Ganley Mountain, it's 1.8

The lone building in the center is the old post office,
all that is left of the Waldorf Mine boomtown.

miles away but nearly flat—so it's pretty quick and easy going (you'll be hiking most of the distance on four-wheel-drive roads).
6.0 Return at the Waldorf Mine.

Notes The Edwards–Ganley traverse is quite enjoyable for several reasons: the mining history, the great views, and the low-work, high-reward aspect of grabbing three peaks in a single outing. Some hikers are put off by the network of four-wheel-drive roads, but most will find they simply add to the character of the area. Ganley is 1.9 miles from McClellan.

If you want to add on a really obscure peak, 12,275-foot Pendleton Mountain can be hiked along the northeast slopes/ridge from Ganley, passing over UN 12,491 in the process. You have to want it, though. It's 1.6 miles one way from Ganley and, of course, 1.6 miles back to the drop point to Waldorf Mine. For style points, it's possible to mountain bike up to Ganley Peak along the roads, then hike over to Pendleton.

10. ✪ Argentine Peak (13,738') to Mount Wilcox (13,408') Loop

Round-Trip Distance	6.6 miles
Class	2
Difficulty	5/10
Hiking Time	4–7 hours
Total Elevation Gain	2,915'

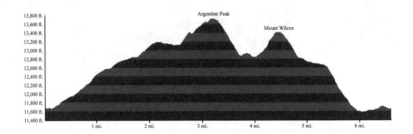

Terrain	Wide trails and four-wheel-drive roads followed by easy, broad slopes between the peaks and back to the basin.
Best Time to Climb	June–October

Overview Argentine Pass and Argentine Peak pay homage to silver, the valuable ore whose elemental symbol is Ag, from the Latin word *argentum* (which means "shining"). Argentine Peak can get very windy. In 1912, winds of 165 miles per hour were recorded—and may have blown even harder, evidenced by the fact those wind speeds destroyed the monitoring equipment. These are very fun, off-trail mountains with easy slopes. Lots of mountain goats call this area home—make sure if you have dogs, they don't antagonize them. As with many of the hikes in this book, there are link-up options, including humble Otter Mountain and a traverse over to Guenella Pass (see additional routes).

Mile/Route 0.0 This route starts the same as Mount Edwards: Head up Argentine Pass 2.1 miles.

2.1 Go off-trail south and follow the north slopes of Argentine Peak 1.0 mile to its often-windy summit.

3.1 Argentine Peak's impressive summit. A stalwart chain of power lines stands between Argentine and Wilcox. Descend east off of Argentine Peak, passing below the power lines at 12,890 feet at the low point of the Argentine–Wilcox saddle. Continue up the southwest ridge slopes of Mount Wilcox.

4.5 Mount Wilcox's summit. The rock here entertains interesting shades of orange and red, courtesy of iron ore and other deposits. Views to the Waldorf Mine, McClellan Mountain, and Ganley Mountain to the north show just how much development once went into this area. It's also a good place to snap a shot of the entire east side of Argentine Pass. The parking area will be visible and the way back will be easy to navigate, assuming you aren't in the thick of foggy storms. Tread off the north slopes and work down into the basin, where a few slightly steeper slopes grant access to the valley floor.

Note: Perhaps it's a personal preference, but I find the north slopes off Mount Wilcox incredibly beautiful. The broad, wide-open terrain decorated with alpine flowers and mountain grasses is quite stunning. The optional walk over to Otter Mountain is 1.8 miles from Wilcox, but you will be hiking 0.8 mile of that anyhow to get down. The additional mile and back of easy walking is worth the time.

Left to right: Grays Peak, Torreys Peak, and Mount Edwards, seen from Mount Wilcox. If you look closely, you can see a truck driving up the middle of Argentine Pass.

6.6 There are a lot of places to safely drop down into the basin, though the sooner you drop off the shoulder of Wilcox, the steeper they will be. Going farther north offers more moderate descent terrain. Return to your vehicle in about 6.6 miles.

Edwards–Grays–Torreys Point-to-Point from Loveland Pass

Class 2+ – 9.7 miles – 5,700' elevation gain

This big day is a ridge walker's dream. Only strong hikers who are ready for the high altitude—it's not a beginner's route. Collect Mount Edwards, Grays Peak, Torreys Peak, Grizzly Peak, and "Cupid" along the way with almost 6,000 feet of elevation gain (most of it gained while hiking over 13,500 feet). The terrain is Class 2+ with the toughest scrambling on the descent of Torreys over to 13,427-foot Grizzly Peak. Park vehicle number two at Loveland Pass (see page 80).

Argentine Pass to Guenella Pass

Class 2 + – 8.1 miles – 3,200' elevation gain

Park a second vehicle at the high point of the paved Guenella Pass (roughly 7.8 miles farther up the pass from the pulloff to Waldorf Mine) and start from Waldorf Mine. Grab Argentine Peak, then go directly south to an unnamed bump in the ridge—look at that, you're on the Continental Divide. Go southeast on the ridges over to the aptly named Square Top Mountain, 13,794 feet, before dropping down its semipopular summit to the ever-busy Guenella Pass parking area.

McClellan–Wilcox Grand Slam

Class 2 – 8.6 miles – 3,810' elevation gain

Yet another reasonable traverse on solid terrain, this is essentially the Argentine–Wilcox loop with a prelude of McClellan and Edwards. Begin by getting McClellan first, then tour above the entire Waldorf Mine Basin, grabbing Edwards, Argentine, and Wilcox. Strong hikers can knock this one out in about 6 hours (or less) thanks to the very solid terrain along the ridgelines.

VII. Stevens Gulch Trailhead (11,260')

Stevens Gulch is by far the most popular trailhead along I-70. On a summer weekend, the parking lot often fills by 6 a.m. with vehicles. By 8 a.m., the access road is lined with parked vehicles. Grays and Torreys Peaks, two 14,000-foot summits, are the feature attractions. They have very well-maintained trails, modest mileage, and spectacular views. Not to be missed are Mount Edwards and Kelso Mountain, also accessible from this area. Kelso Ridge on Torreys Peak may be the best Class 3 ridge scramble in the Front Range. Baker Mountain out of Grizzly Gulch is only for those who love steep, off-trail hikes.

PEAKS

- Torreys Peak: 14,267'
- Grays Peak: 14,270'
- Kelso Mountain: 13,164'
- Mount Edwards: 13,850'
- McClellan Mountain: 13,587'
- Baker Mountain: 12,448'

Wilderness Area and Range

Arapaho National Forest, Front Range

Trailhead Distance from I-70

3.1 miles

Driving Directions

Take Exit 221 for Bakerville. If exiting westbound, go left under I-70 and arrive at a large dirt parking area and the start of the Stevens Gulch Road (Forest Service Road 321). Exiting eastbound, simply turn right into the dirt lot. The dirt road to the Stevens Gulch Trailhead is straight ahead to the south. It is 3 miles to the trailhead. This road is bumpy, slightly steep in sections, but a *carefully driven passenger car can safely manage the first mile and possibly beyond.* One mile in is the turnoff to Grizzly Gulch to the right and ample room for parking—a good idea if you don't want to test your passenger car. SUCs, SUVs, and four-wheel drives can carry on for 2 more miles to the official trailhead.

This road used to be passable for all vehicles—and may still be in coming years. However, several large avalanche slides and very heavy usage have rutted out the road in sections. High clearance is a good idea, though nearly every summer day you'll see a few Honda Accords and the like at the trailhead. The road is right on the edge of being passable by cars . . . use caution. There will be a few private driveways up until the boundary of the parking area—please do not park on private land. If you're going on a summer weekend, expect the entire lot to be filled by 6:30 a.m. Any later than that and you'll likely be parking along the road.

Vehicle Recommendations

While plenty of cars make it to the trailhead, many passenger cars will bottom out in the steep sections. The road never gets super steep or rocky,

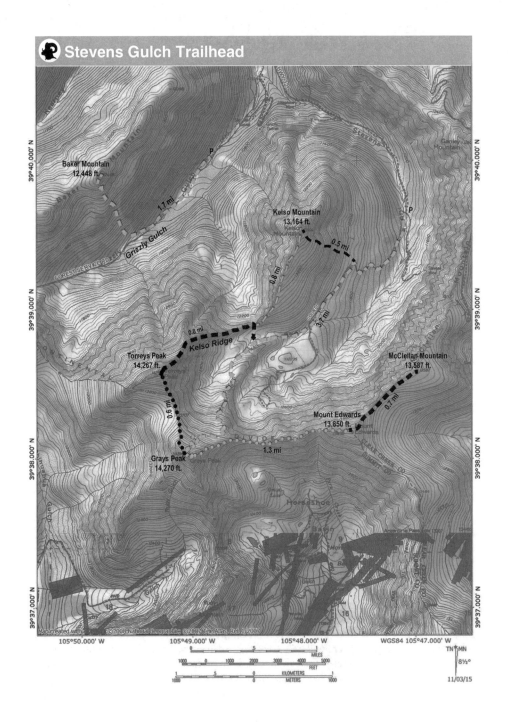

Baker Mountain
12,448 ft.

1.7 mi

Grizzly Gulch

FOREST SERVICE RD

P

Kelso Mountain
13,164 ft.

0.5 mi

P

0.8 mi

3.7 mi

0.8 mi

Kelso Ridge

Torreys Peak
14,267 ft.

McClellan Mountain
13,587 ft.

0.7 mi

0.6 mi

Mount Edwards
13,850 ft.

DIVIDE

1.3 mi

Grays Peak
14,270 ft.

Horseshoe

39°40.000' N

39°39.000' N

39°38.000' N

39°37.000' N

105°50.000' W   105°49.000' W   105°48.000' W   WGS84 105°47.000' W

MILES
1000   0   1000   2000   3000   4000   5000
FEET

KILOMETERS
1000   0   1000
METERS

TN MN
8½°

11/03/15

so SUVs/SUCs do just fine. No matter what vehicle you are driving, some years driving to the trailhead is impossible due to big avalanche paths that can block the road until mid-June.

Fees/Camping There are no fees to hike or camp, though please be careful not to camp on private land. On busy weekends, camping in the unimproved sites along Grizzly Gulch is an option that is sometimes less crowded (and about 1,000 vertical feet lower).

Note: This entire stretch from the bottom of the road to the trailhead has gotten overused in the past few years. There's a lot of trash in the woods at camp spots, and the lack of restrooms along Grizzly Gulch has made the close forests rather disgusting. When you visit, please try extra hard to minimize your impact. This area used to be pristine wilderness.

Dog Regulations Dogs are allowed on leash, though if your pup isn't good with kids, crowds, or other dogs, this isn't the trail for him (or consider hiking in September or October when the crowds decrease).

Summary You can't fault people for visiting Stevens Gulch—the peaks and routes from this area are very close to the Denver metro area and are excellent day hikes. Many people hike Grays and Torreys as their first fourteeners. Others use these as training peaks, and it's not unusual to meet folks who have summited many times already. Throughout the summer, this is a very busy place. Over 300 people may be aiming for summit on any given July day. The overwhelming majority of hikers are sticking to the main Grays Peak trail and traversing to Torreys Peak. Kelso Mountain, Mount Edwards, and McClellan Mountain are all but forgotten. Kelso Ridge, a Class 3 scramble on Torreys Peak, may be the best moderate scramble in the Front Range, featuring an exciting, brief knife-edge section just before the finish.

Primary Routes

11. ✪ Grays Peak (14,270') and Torreys Peak (14,267')

Round-Trip Distance	8 miles
Class	2
Difficulty	4/10
Hiking Time	5–8 hours
Total Elevation Gain	3,600'
Terrain	Well-worn and easy-to-follow trails.
Best Time to Climb	Mid-June–October

Overview This extremely popular route starts over 11,000 feet. Stevens Gulch has an interesting mining history, and many of the ruins still populate the valley floor. The way up to Grays Peak (usually the first summit in the pairing) is as straightforward as it gets—just follow the trail. Torreys is a little over 0.6 mile away from the summit of Grays. The low point between the traverse

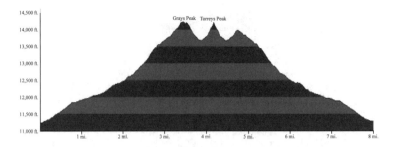

goes down to 13,707 feet before climbing 513 feet to Torreys summit. A shortcut trail from the saddle eliminates the need to revisit Grays summit. An early start beats the crowds and the afternoon thunderstorms.

Mile/Route **0.0** At the large trailhead kiosk, cross over a sturdy bridge and begin your adventure. The trail is wide and easy to follow. Enjoy the views as it twists into the valley. Grays and Torreys are stunning from this vantage, while humble Mount Edwards barely appears as a rounded bump on the ridge to the south. Kelso Mountain's large dome dominates the northern views at the start.

2.1 The trail begins to ascend a small ridge before getting steeper toward the shoulder of Grays Peak. After hitting the broad shoulder, the trail switchbacks up to the summit of Grays Peak.

3.7 Welcome to the highest point in the Front Range (by 3 feet over Torreys) and the 10th highest peak in Colorado. The summit of Grays Peak has enough room to handle the crowds—find a spot and soak in the views. The way to Torreys couldn't be more obvious. Follow an access trail north off Grays to your second fourteener of the day 0.6 mile away.

4.0 The saddle between Grays and Torreys. Torreys looms ahead.

4.3 Torreys summit. Kelso Ridge to the east looks tough from this point of view. Return the way you came, back to the saddle and taking a short connector trail to regain the Grays Peak trail.

8.0 Finish. Mileage may be slightly less than 8 miles if you took a more direct route up Grays (via the shoulder) or Torreys (avoided switchbacks).

Notes Almost entirely forgotten is the fun Grays to Edwards (and McClellan Mountain) option. It's 1.3 miles from Grays to Edwards. See the additional routes later in this chapter for details. Those who prefer a good scramble will love Kelso Ridge as the start to this pair, grabbing Torreys first and then walking over to Grays. For those who are curious, the south ridge of Grays to Ruby Mountain to the south is Class 3 with some route-finding required to avoid downclimbing Class 4 terrain. A really nice loop (not covered in this book) starts from Horseshoe Basin south of Grays Peak and gets the east ridge of Ruby Mountain, then climbs the south ridge of Grays Peak, and traverses to Mount Edwards before looping down the west side of Argentine Pass—almost 5,000 feet of elevation gain over 8.5 miles.

Kelso Ridge

This excellent scramble takes the direct east ridge of Torreys 0.8 mile to the summit. From a distance, it looks like it may be a technical climb, but up close it reveals its secrets. There is some short-lived dramatic exposure toward the end of the ridge.

Start on the Grays Peak Trail. Around 1.8 miles in, start trending toward the saddle between Kelso Mountain and Torreys Peak (there are a few climber's trails). Check out the old mining building just below the pass on your way up. Gain the saddle at 12,400 feet and get ready. It's 1,867 vertical feet in 0.7 mile to the top. Scrambles are on mostly solid rock. There are optional climbs that can be averted by route-finding the easier Class 3 terrain on the right (north) side of the ridge in most cases. The crux of the climb is at 14,000 feet when the summit is within a Frisbee's throw away—the fabled knife-edge. It's not long—only about 12 feet, followed by a scramble down to a large, white quartz block to the top of the Dead Dog couloir. Those who don't like exposure will have to suck it up to reach the top. The short walk to the summit of Torreys after this is a snap. Descend via the standard route or tack on Grays on the way home.

Nearing the summit of Torreys Peak after clearing the knife-edge on Kelso Ridge

Kelso Mountain via "Torreys Ridge"

Class 2 – 5.8 miles – 1,960' elevation gain

"Torreys Ridge" is the waggish name for the broad, south ridge of Kelso Mountain. Follow the directions to the Kelso–Torreys saddle, except this time go north 0.8 mile along easy off-trail terrain to the summit of Kelso. The craggy cliffs off the west side of the ridge stand in contrast to the moderate slopes on the east side. After topping out, you can save time by heading directly down the steep, grassy slopes of Kelso. Those same east slopes are notorious avalanche traps come late autumn to late spring, so if there's snow, play it safe and return to the saddle.

Grays–Edwards–McClellan Mountain

Class 2/3 – 11.7 miles – 4,250' elevation gain

After summiting Grays however you wish, head over and grab Mount Edwards. If you add Torreys via Kelso Ridge (a fine idea), the route is upgraded to Class 3. Mount Edwards is 1.3 miles along a Class 2+ ridge that has some fun scrambling. McClellan Mountain is 0.7 mile from Edwards. Most people get these two peaks from Waldorf Mine (see page 46). Unfortunately, there's no easy way down from these peaks back into Stevens Gulch until returning to the Grays Peak Trail. The Goatfinger Couloir is too loose and steep to be a good summer descent route.

The start of Kelso Ridge as dawn breaks

The Stevens Slam: Kelso to Edwards

Class 3 – 9.1 miles – 5,260' elevation gain

This is one of those fun, challenging routes that *someone is bound to take too seriously and try to set a world-record time on.* To each their own, I suppose. Regardless of your motivation, this is a heck of a big day. Start by chugging up the east slopes of Kelso Mountain, then descend the saddle and ascend Kelso Ridge to Torreys. Traverse to Grays and over to Edwards, then return via the Grays Peak Trail. Four good peaks all over 13,000 feet in one outing and nearly a mile of elevation gained—this one isn't for beginners!

Baker Mountain (12,448') via Grizzly Gulch

Class 2+ – 2.4 miles – 1,740' elevation gain

Baker Mountain is even more forgotten than Kelso. To get started on this route, drive 1.0 mile up the Stevens Gulch Road and take the right turnoff down Grizzly Gulch. SUCs, SUVs, and four-wheel drives can make it down the to the parking 1.0 mile in. Passenger cars driven with care can make it here—or close to it. While the four-wheel-drive road continues across a river crossing there, this is a good place to park (just before the crossing). The road splits here; stay right across the river crossing. If you have a four-wheel drive, you can bash up this road a bit farther, but the hike isn't bad.

From the parking area, go 0.9 mile west along the road (Forest Service Road 189.C), where the broad, loose, south slopes of Baker will be exposed. Most people who come this far are aiming for the north-facing Tuning Fork snow route on Torreys Peak. For Baker, however, turn up and follow a gash caused by an avalanche path to the summit 0.8 mile straight up. Baker's summit is 12,448 feet and is a short distance from where the avalanche path ends.

Besides the novelty of hiking an obscure peak, this route can make the start of an interesting point-to-point west to "Cupid," the unofficial name of Colorado's 555th highest mountain (see Loveland Pass, page 80). From there, it's an easy traverse over and down to Loveland Pass, where vehicle number two will park. This point-to-point is 4.9 miles but goes over 3,000 vertical feet.

Even More Options!

Stevens Gulch has some big point-to-point options, though the driving aspects of connecting to some, like Waldorf Mine, make it a pain to set up the vehicles. However, big traverses to Guenella Pass (Grays, Edwards, Argentine, Square Top) and Loveland Pass (Torreys, Grizzly, "Cupid") are feasible. A Torreys, Grizzly, Lenawee traverse ending at A-Basin is another unique route, though the terrain between Grizzly and Lenawee is likely Class 4 (or hard Class 3).

The takeaway is that there is a lot of fun to be had out of Stevens Gulch besides just the standard Grays and Torreys route. And if you aren't up for summits, just touring the valley mining operations makes for an interesting day.

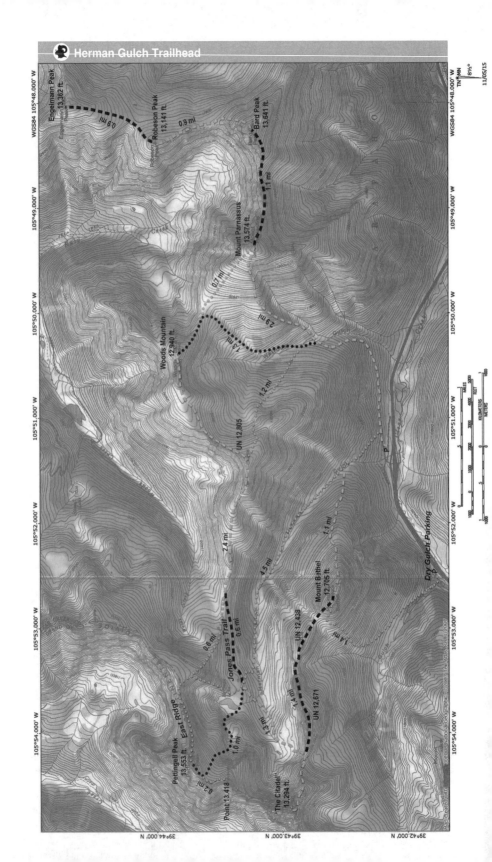

Herman Gulch Trailhead

Engelmann Peak 13,362 ft.

Robeson Peak 13,141 ft.

Bard Peak 13,641 ft.

Mount Parnassus 13,574 ft.

Woods Mountain 12,940 ft.

UN 12,305

Pettingell Peak 13,553 ft.

East Ridge

Jones Pass Trail

Point 13,418

"The Citadel" 13,294 ft.

UN 12,671

UN 12,438

Mount Bethel 12,705 ft.

Dry Gulch Parking

0.9 mi
0.9 mi
1.1 mi
0.7 mi
2.9 mi
4.3 mi
1.2 mi
2.4 mi
0.6 mi
0.6 mi
1.0 mi
0.2 mi
1.3 mi
4.5 mi
1.1 mi
4.4 mi
1.4 mi

WGS84 105°48.000' W
105°49.000' W
105°50.000' W
105°51.000' W
105°52.000' W
105°53.000' W
105°54.000' W

39°44.000' N
39°43.000' N
39°42.000' N

TN MN
8½°
11/05/15

MILES
KILOMETERS
FEET
METERS

VIII. Herman Gulch Trailhead (10,270')

Welcome to summit hiker's heaven. This trailhead is extremely popular with day hikers, most of whom are out for a stroll to Herman Lake and never set foot on a single mountaintop. None of the summits in this area have formal trails, but all of them are worthy adventures. Hikers make a decision early in their day: go west to Herman Gulch or east to Watrous Gulch . . . or link up the two gulches via an inconspicuous summit between the two. Two excellent Class 3 routes and several Class 2 walk-ups make this a trailhead you'll revisit many times.

PEAKS

- Woods Mountain: 12,940'
- Pettingell Peak: 13,553'
- "The Citadel": 13,294'
- Mount Bethel: 12,705'
- UN 12,805: 12,805'
- Mount Parnassus: 13,574'

- Bard Peak: 13,641'
- Robeson Peak: 13,141'
- Engelmann Peak: 13,362'
- UN 12,671: 12,671'
- UN 12,438: 12,438'
- Point 13,418: 13,418'

Wilderness Area and Range

Arapaho National Forest/Front Range

Trailhead Distance from I-70

0.1 mile

Driving Directions

Westbound take Exit 218. At the end of the exit, take a sharp right onto the dirt road and proceed a few hundred feet to parking. Eastbound, it's Exit 218, left off the ramp and under I-70, then right after the westbound exit to the same place. There's a restroom at the trailhead, a rarity for most of these routes.

Vehicle Recommendations

Any vehicle can make the trailhead, though the dirt road tends to get rutted when there's rain or snow.

Fees/Camping

There are no fees to hike or camp in this area.

Dog Regulations

Dogs are allowed on leash or under voice control.

Summary

So much hiking, so little time. The most overlooked route in this area is Pettingell Peak's fantastic east ridge, a 0.6-mile Class 3 adventure that compares favorably to Torreys Peak's Kelso Ridge (see page 59), minus the knife-edge. Mount Parnassus is an enormous dome of earth that has a great ghost forest to pass through and the option of linking up to three other peaks. Woods Mountain to UN 12,805 is a great circuit that connects the two gulches (and can be hiked either way). And . . . you guessed it . . . this is a great trailhead to link point-to-point adventures to the 7:30 Mine Trail, Dry Gulch, or Loveland Tunnel West.

Primary Routes

12. ✪ Mount Parnassus (13,574') and Bard Peak (13,641')

Round-Trip Distance	8.3 miles
Class	2
Difficulty	6/10
Hiking Time	6–8 hours
Total Elevation Gain	4,870'
Terrain	Trail fades away to solid, steady, off-trail grassy slopes.
Best Time to Climb	June–October

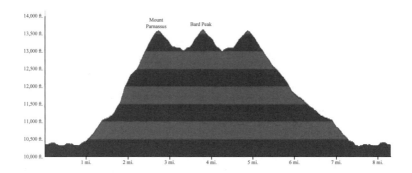

Overview While Parnassus and Bard lack the clout of neighboring Grays and Torreys Peaks, these two thirteeners make for an excellent day hike with a good variety of terrain along the way. Ascend through the ghost forests on Parnassus's western slopes and top out on one of the Front Range's best-kept secrets—the perspectives from the summit are glorious. The traverse over to Bard Peak follows firm grass and rock slopes. From its summit, look east to Silver Plume, Sherman, and Republican Mountains. If you want to test your mountain endurance, tack on Robeson and Engelmann Peaks for some serious extra credit.

Mile/Route 0.0 From the sign kiosk at the trailhead, start along the trail. You'll be making a critical turn in less than 5 minutes into this hike.
0.2 Shortly into the hike, this initial trail comes to a split. Take a right toward Watrous Gulch (this split used to be marked by a sign that was absent in 2016; I hope it is replaced by the time you arrive). The path ascends through a rooted, shady trail.

1.0 A weathered sign announces a split to the Bard Creek Trail, which is little more than a whisper into the woods. Stay on the main, well-worn trail north into Watrous Gulch Basin.

1.6 As the grandeur of Watrous Gulch begins to open up, the lower western slopes of Parnassus reveal themselves to be populated by a forest of gnarled, twisted bristlecone pine trees. Leave the trail, hop over the gulch, and begin the steady grind up the slopes at 11,200 feet. It is 1.3 miles up and 2,374 vertical feet up from here.

2.1 The spooky, twisted trunks gradually give way to sparse shrubs and then, around 12,300 feet, comes the end of timberline. Carry onward. Views of the gulch below are mesmerizing.

2.9 The well-earned summit of Mount Parnassus. Many hikers find that the effort up Parnassus was more work than anticipated. Bear in mind that it will be 1,370 feet of additional work to summit Bard and return to Parnassus. Head east toward Bard Peak, staying slightly south of the main ridge for better footing.

3.5 12,939 feet and the saddle between Parnassus and Bard. Oh goody, only 732 vertical feet to the summit. Get cracking!

4.0 The summit of Bard Peak! Strong hikers craving a big day can prep for the traverse to Robeson and Engelmann Peaks. See the "Notes" for details on this traverse, which adds 3.6 total miles and 1,627 more vertical feet to your day. Otherwise, return back up to the summit of Parnassus.

5.1 Back at the summit of Parnassus. For the descent, it's easier on the knees to go off the northwest shoulder of Parnassus and follow the slopes

Looking at Bard Peak from Mount Parnassus

to the faint but visible Watrous Gulch Trail. It adds a slight bit of mileage but ultimately saves time. If you don't initially see the trail in the valley, just aim for the stream running through the gulch. The trail is just beside it.

6.5 Arrive back at the valley floor somewhere around this mileage (depending on how directly you descended Parnassus). Regain the Watrous Gulch trail and follow it home. Afternoon light in this basin is often incredible, lighting up the willows, yellow grasses, and wildflowers.

8.3 Finish.

Notes   The walk over to Robeson Peak, 13,141 feet, is 0.9 mile from Bard Peak. The saddle between Bard and Robeson is at its best in late summer, when the grasses turn deep crimson and vermillion hues. Wind explodes up the steep saddle cliffs many days—be ready! It is another 0.9 mile along these easy, seldom-visited slopes to visit Engelmann Peak, 13,362 feet. Its summit is a mix of red and green grasses, wildflowers, and swaths of shining white quartz.

All told, this full four-pack makes for a huge day—6,430 feet of elevation gain over 12 miles. But it's a fair hike; the footing is solid, the ridges are easy to follow, and it remains Class 2 throughout. There's no easy way to get Robeson and Engelmann (the old standards from the north pass private mine land), so this is as good a time as any to get them. You'll realize for yourself you can skip revisiting Robeson on the return—just skirt to the east.

And if you are a hiking maniac, 12,940-foot Woods Mountain can be a fifth summit if you traverse there from Parnassus on the return.

13. ✪ Pettingell Peak (13,553')–East Ridge

Round-Trip Distance	8.9 miles
Class	3
Difficulty	8/10
Hiking Time	6–8 hours
Total Elevation Gain	3,260'
Terrain	Class 1 trail leads to steep ridges and ultimately a fun, challenging Class 3 ridge on mostly solid rock.
Best Time to Climb	June–October

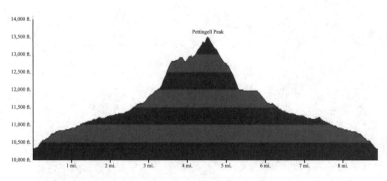

Overview Pettingell Peak is the highest point of Grand County. While it does have a rather tame Class 2 route up its south slopes, the Class 3 east ridge is where the action is. From a distance, the ridge looks to present some harrowing difficulties, but up close the way through reveals itself. This is an excellent introduction to route-finding on Class 3 terrain (and for fourteener fans, a nice primer for ridges like Capitol Peak). It's never wildly exposed—in fact, less so than its counterpart on Torreys Peak, Kelso Ridge.

Mile/Route 0.0 Start at the sign kiosk and head up the trail to a split.

0.2 Take the left trail west toward Herman Lake. Enjoy the warm-up walk; you'll be on it for a few miles to start your day. The trail is well traveled and easy to follow.

3.0 As you close in on Herman Lake, you'll emerge above treeline and reach a trail split. You have two options: Go right on the Jones Pass trail and gain the ridgeline there, or continue up a bit farther and scramble more directly up a loose, rocky spur to gain the ridge. The Jones Pass option adds about a mile extra, but may be quicker since it gets on the ridge proper and slopes more easily. That said, the "spur scramble" is steep and more direct—and you're here to scramble, right? This route follows the spur line.

3.1 Before reaching Herman Lake, leave the trail around 12,100 feet and ascend the south-facing spur that will lead to the east ridge. The rock here is loose in places, so test everything. The Class 3 sections are just before topping out on a broad, flat plateau.

High on Pettingell's east ridge, with Herman Lake far below

3.6 Finally atop the ridge proper at 12,930 feet; the east ridge beckons. Several sections look quite imposing from here, especially a devious notch toward the end of the ridge. Never fear. As mentioned, the best lines will reveal themselves as you proceed. Drop down into a narrow saddle and head west 0.9 mile from there to the summit. Begin the ridge by staying left (south) of the first steep rock outcrops, then gain the ridge proper again. Class 4 aficionados can surf the ridge the entire time, but there are some tricky downclimbs to be aware of.

4.0 After you bypass the initial scramble, the ridge mellows out for a time. Continue along Class 3 terrain on mostly good rock. The notch continues to look like a vexing problem.

4.3 Top out on a small bump in the ridge—time to confront the notch! Once at its base, the scramble up is suddenly very manageable. Either go directly up or slightly left, both solid Class 3 options. Above the notch is a wildflower carpet that graciously leads to an easy walk over to the summit.

4.5 Pettingell's welcome summit! To descend, follow the broad, sometimes steep southeast slopes toward Herman Lake. If there's snow, this is a great place to glissade and save time. There are a few cliffs prior to the last short descent to Herman Lake; they can be avoided by following the stream that flows down between them. When you reach them, it's easy enough to avoid downclimbing this difficult section—just walk a few feet over and find the more mellow terrain to descend.

5.5 Loop around the south side of Herman Lake and regain the main trail. Follow it back to the trailhead, likely passing scores of hikers on the way back.

8.9 Finish.

Midway along Pettingell's Class 3 ridge

Notes Point 13,418 is an interesting scramble to a block guarded by a brief notch along Pettingell's south ridge. It's 0.3 mile from the summit. Note the traverse beyond along the south ridge to "The Citadel" gets into Class 4 and 5 terrain, so unless you are equipped for technical climbing, head back down.

Pettingell Peak can be directly climbed by the southeast slopes as a Class 2 route—it's a favorite among springtime skiers for its consistent grade. It's also a good option if you want your dog to join in the summit day (no dogs on Class 3 terrain is my personal rule).

14. ✪ Woods Mountain (12,940')–UN 12,805 Double Gulch Tour

Round-Trip Distance	9.3 miles
Class	2
Difficulty	6.5/10
Hiking Time	6–8 hours
Total Elevation Gain	3,100'
Terrain	Trail leads to off-trail, firm, grassy slopes, eventually joining an established trail to finish.
Best Time to Climb	June–October

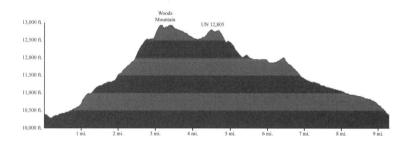

Overview Author's confession: UN 12,805 is my favorite unnamed summit in the Front Range. The walk over from Woods Mountain is charming, thanks to the wildflowers and snowfields that decorate the broad ridge. Views from UN 12,805 extend down to the busy highway and Pettingell Peak looks majestic when looking head on at the east ridge. North of Woods Mountain is Red Mountain, a tempting peak that is unfortunately on private mining land. This loop connects with the Jones Pass Trail and returns via Herman Gulch, connecting it to Watrous Gulch.

Mile/Route 0.0 From the kiosk, head up the prominent trail into the woods.

0.2 At the split, go right and head toward Watrous Gulch (just like the start of the Mount Parnassus hike). Rather than split off the trail, however, this route follows the Watrous Gulch Trail to its northern terminus at the foot of Woods Mountain.

1.0 Stay left on the well-worn Watrous Gulch Trail at the junction with the Bard Creek Trail. Continue north into the basin. Slowly, the basin opens up to alpine meadows and pockets of willows. A few easy stream crossings intersect the trail.

2.3 Just as the trail approaches treeline at 11,700 feet, it fades away. No problem, as the layout of the peaks is visually clear. After a final pocket of shrubs and low krummholz, begin the push up Woods's south slopes. Staying slightly right is the path of least resistance to the ridge.

3.2 After gaining the ridge, turn west up to the rocky bench that is the summit of Woods Mountain. The option to stay in Watrous Gulch and chug up Mount Parnassus is available. For the full tour, descend west off Woods Mountain toward a prominent bump to the southwest—UN 12,805. The walk over is pleasant, and the views remain stellar throughout the traverse.

4.4 The friendly summit of UN 12,805 appreciates your company. Looking due west, you'll see the way back is laid out before you. Follow the ridge down, where a hiker's trail will materialize and lead down to the Jones Pass Trail at a low point on the ridge.

5.6 Take the Jones Pass Trail left (south) for a few minutes and connect with the Herman Lake Trail. Since you're only 0.2 mile from the lake, it's a nice place to grab a snack and take a break before returning. When you are ready, take the Herman Lake Trail back east to the trailhead.

9.3 Finish.

Notes This route can be done in reverse. The reverse loop's descent off Woods into Watrous Gulch is steeper than the drop off UN 12,805, but certainly not terrible. Watrous to Herman, as stated previously, is the more logical loop. If you're entertaining the thought of staying on the east ridge to Pettingell Peak—a very big day—make sure you start predawn to avoid afternoon storms. The east ridge is no-man's-land if mother nature decides to throw thundershowers your way.

Additional Routes

"The Citadel" (13,294')

Class 3 – 8.7 miles – 3,220' elevation gain

This classic route follows the Herman Lake Trail 3.0 miles, then drops off-trail southwest across the valley floor and up to Fortress saddle. From there, it's a stiff push west up steep terrain followed by passing under the summit towers to the south. After passing a few shadowy gullies, a small, sandy notch on the west side of the ridge reveals itself. Scamper up to a narrow gap that splits the twin summits of "The Citadel"—Class 3 scrambles go to both the east and west summits 4.3 miles in. Return the way you came. "The Citadel" is also covered on page 79 as an ascent route from Dry Gulch.

UN 12,671, UN 12,438, and Mount Bethel (12,705')

Class 2 – 7.1 miles – 3,400' elevation gain

This route follows the same path to Fortress saddle as "The Citadel," except at the saddle it goes east rather than west. It traverses over the trio of

Looking west toward Pettingell Peak (center) and "The Citadel" (left) and into Dry Gulch

summits, ending at Mount Bethel 1.4 miles past the saddle. The most logical way down, though a bit steep, is to descend off Bethel's northeast slopes back to Herman Gulch for a nice 7.1-mile loop. Another interesting option is to make this a point-to-point with one vehicle parked at Dry Gulch (see page 72)—the descent down Bethel is steep but only 1.4 miles (6.8 total miles) and passes the big line of snow fences.

Other Point-to-Points
Point-to-points can connect the 7:30 Mine Trail via Bard Peak (see page 39), the Bard Creek Trailhead (see page 32), the Dry Gulch Trailhead (see page 72), or the Loveland Tunnel West Trailhead (see page 88).

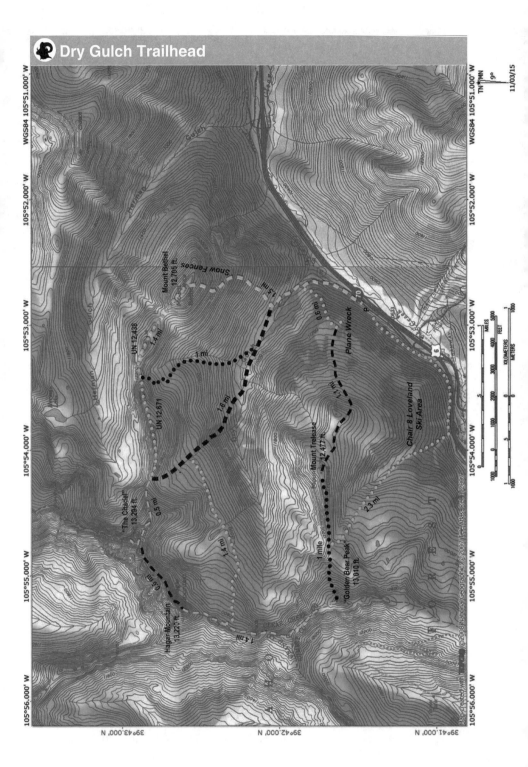

Dry Gulch Trailhead

IX. Dry Gulch Trailhead (10,600')

Dry Gulch has access to two unique destinations that aren't summits: a field of airplane wreckage and the towering line of snow fences on Mount Bethel. Nearly all the summits in this area are hard earned, either from the steepness of the slopes or the scrambling required to reach their tops. Also, don't expect there to be trails beyond the initial access road—though navigation tends to be straightforward. Loops to Loveland Ski Area's peaks or up and over to the Loveland Tunnel West parking area are options.

PEAKS

- Mount Bethel: 12,705'
- Hagar Mountain: 13,220'
- Mount Trelease: 12,477'
- "Golden Bear Peak": 13,010'

- "The Citadel": 13,294'
- UN 12,438: 12,438'
- UN 12,671: 12,671'

Wilderness Area and Range

Arapaho National Forest, Front Range

Trailhead Distance from I-70

Less than 100 feet from the highway

Driving Directions

From westbound I-70, take Exit 216. At the end of the exit ramp, take a hairpin right onto a dirt access road. Continue for a few hundred feet to a gated area. Park here to the side of the gate along the road. From eastbound I-70, take Exit 216, turn left at the end of the exit, and then take your next left. Drive under I-70 and head toward the westbound exit and pass it, taking the dirt access road.

Vehicle Recommendations All vehicles.

Fees/Camping There are no fees to hike or camp.

Dog Regulations Quadruple vigilance getting out at the trailhead. You are literally within spitting distance of I-70 West, so leash those puppies up until you are a ways up the trail.

Summary The airplane wreckage on the slopes of Mount Trelease is a part of Colorado's mountain aviation history. If you visit, please be respectful and leave all debris. Mount Bethel is a direct push straight up, making the presence of the large line of snow fences that more impressive. The summit views of Mount Bethel west into Dry Gulch make a good case for being the best vantage in the Front Range. "The Citadel" is a good, tough Class 3 summit and strong hikers will love the Class 3 connecting ridge over to Hagar Mountain. Even though the distances are short, these hikes can make for a long day.

15. ✪ Mount Bethel (12,705') and Plane Wreck Detour

Round-Trip Distance	4 miles
Class	2
Difficulty	6.5/10
Hiking Time	4–6 hours
Total Elevation Gain	2,680'
Terrain	Steep, sustained grassy slopes.
Best Time to Climb	June–October

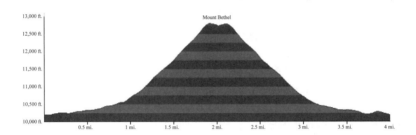

Overview This combo hike makes a detour to see the wreckage field before making a direct push to the summit of Mount Bethel. A word of warning on the airplane wreckage: it's not just formless, twisted metal. There are many identifiable objects and personal belongings in the debris. The crash occurred on October 2, 1970, and many parts of the Martin 404 are still quite intact. See "Notes" on page 77 for more information on the crash. Mount Bethel is a good test of a hiker's vertical power—nearly 2,000 feet straight up. Thankfully, the slopes have good footing up, provided there's no snow. The snow fences along the way are there to prevent avalanches from sliding down onto I-70 and are quite impressive in person.

Mile/Route 0.0 From the gate, head northeast up the wide access road. At 0.4 mile, you'll come to a flat spot where the road will cross Dry Gulch Creek. There is a large, fenced-in storage area to the right. Just before the fenced area, there is an area on the left side of the road (before the creek) that looks like an old parking area with a path headed uphill into the trees. This is the informal trail to the wreck site. This steep hill was cut to reach the wreck site in 1970. Leave the main road and head up this slope to the west.

From the start of this path, you are less than half a mile from the crash site. The route goes up about 600 vertical feet in a short distance. Stay on this unmarked trail as it climbs through the woods. About midway up, there is a cairn that seems to point to a very faint trail. I assume this is a shortcut to the wreck, though I would advise skipping it and staying on the main trail.

About 0.8 mile in from the parking area, the steep trail will flatten out just past a bit of a marshy area on your left. At this point, the trail seems to faintly go both left (downhill) and straight through some trees. You'll want to follow the left path, which is unmarked and could be overgrown—for a moment, you will likely be off-trail. A few faint hiker's trails fade in from the woods. If you are a bit confused, just remember to aim left (south) downhill after the steep section of the trail levels off.

By taking this path, you'll approach the wreck in a few hundred feet from above. The area is cleared of trees and at first it's difficult to tell if you are looking at downed, gray timber or metal. Upon closer inspection, the breadth of the carnage will become apparent. Almost 50 years after the October 2, 1970, crash, gnarled aluminum and crumpled metal gears are eerily unrusted. There are several memorial objects, including a tombstone with a Wichita State football helmet and a few faded flags with the names of the victims. After you have paid your respects, return to the road, which will put your mileage at about 1.4 miles by the time you get back to the main road.

1.4 Back on the road, head up and past the fenced-in storage area and follow the road as it bends west into Dry Gulch. Mount Bethel is looming to the north. After the bend in the road, leave it and head . . . straight up. There are no trails up, but the navigation is easy. There are a few patches of forest and shrubs, and the slope is broad with good footing. Up you go!

The plane wreckage on the side of Mount Trelease is extensive.

Grinding up past the trademark snow fences

2.0 A high, forested patch has a bit of level land with discrete nooks to set up a tent—if you want to lug one up. The snow fences are just past this patch. They are considerably longer and taller up close than they seem from below. The left (west) fence is the logical one to follow to the summit.

2.5 After passing the snow fences, chug up to a false summit. Don't fret; the true summit is about 100 feet west with barely any additional elevation gain. Views here are just . . . wow. "The Citadel" and Hagar Mountain look foreboding and fearsome to the northwest. Dry Gulch expands out to "Golden Bear Peak" directly west, and the Gore Range peeks out from behind it. Herman Gulch and Pettingell Peak stand to the north, and the huge dome of Mount Parnassus is due east. Loveland Ski Area and Loveland Pass are to the south.

Return down the slopes for a direct shot back to the parking area—or make the walk over to UN 12,438. This rounded high point on the ridge will feel like a pure summit once it is under your boots. The same can be said for its neighbor, UN 12,671. The saddle between these two features a nice little creek that can be followed back to the access road (which is easily visible from above). UN 12,438 is 0.5 mile from Bethel's summit; UN 12,671 is 1.1 miles from Bethel. From UN 12,671, it is about 2 miles back to the trailhead, for a 5.6-mile round-trip.

4.0 Finish.

Notes If you decline the wreckage visit, the up and down of Bethel is less than 3 miles round-trip but a burly day. Hiking poles are recommended. Grinding up the slopes to the top is tough but never exposed, and the earth beneath your feet is solid grass with a few firm rocks in the mix. There are plenty of paths to descend from Bethel, and the navigation is easy.

The plane wreck on Mount Trelease carried the Wichita State football team and had 37 total passengers on board, including crew. Only 6 people survived. The cause of the wreck was pilot error. While trying to get a better view of the mountains, the plane became trapped in the box canyon and couldn't pull out in time. There are yearly memorials placed on the day of the crash.

To see photos of the wreck and this entire hike, visit the author's trip report at mountainouswords.com/mountain-air/wichita-state-plane-wreck-mount-bethel-dry-gulch.

Views from the summit of Mount Bethel down into Dry Gulch
are stunning, even by Colorado mountain standards.

Tour of the Unnamed Peaks

Class 2 – 5.7 miles – 2,380' elevation gain

The two high points between Mount Bethel and Fortress saddle have a lot of character, despite not being formal summits. This route is an alternative to reaching them after going up the standard Mount Bethel Route.

Rather than detouring from the main road up Bethel's south slopes, stay on the Dry Gulch road. It will pare down from a two-lane road to a single hiking trail as it heads up into dense pockets of pine trees. Eventually, what passes for a trail will dissolve in the woods about 1.2 miles in. At 1.7 miles, an unnamed creek (how fitting) signals a good place to head up toward Fortress saddle. At times, this stream looks like it was laid by master artisans thanks to the rocks piled neatly on its perimeter. Above treeline, the true beauty of this route reveals itself.

Reaching the first summit, UN 12,671 is a lot of fun. Rather than go to the saddle, a nice option is to play around on the easy scrambles on the south side of the ridge to gain the summit. There are walk-arounds to all the boulders and rock outcrops, so it's never technical unless you want it to be. Top out around 2.7 miles. From here, either descend back into the gulch off UN 12,671's east ridge and south slopes or continue over to UN 12,438 (about 3.5 miles). Descent of these steep, grassy slopes is possible nearly anywhere you like. Adding on Bethel is possible too (0.5 mile away). Follow the slopes of your choice back to the valley floor and back to the trailhead.

Mount Trelease (12,477')– "Golden Bear Peak" (13,010') Traverse

Class 2 – 5.8 miles – 2,560' elevation gain

This route is most enjoyable as a loop that descends in bounds of Loveland Ski Area to Chair 8 (rather than return through the thick woods in Dry Gulch). As with many of the routes in this guide, it can be combined with other peaks or done as a point-to-point with a second vehicle waiting at the Loveland Tunnel West trailhead (see page 88).

Start the route by going 0.4 mile up the road from the parking area, then take the left into the woods toward the plane wreck site, as mentioned in the Mount Bethel–Plane Wreck hike description. Rather than head south toward the wreckage, stay in the thick of the woods and stay due west, always moving uphill. This requires a bit of navigational savvy and the first mile will be the toughest. After about 1.2 miles, treeline will begin to fade out. The ridge continues up and over Mount Trelease 2.0 miles in (a small shoulder of ridge); then you carry on to 13,010-foot "Golden Bear Peak" roughly 3 miles in. Loveland Ski Area will be to the left of the ridge, Dry Gulch to the right.

While it's possible to descend back into Dry Gulch, the navigation down through the trees can be tricky. A good option is to return via the Loveland Ski Area slopes down to Chair 8, which basically offers a bona fide trail back to I-70. A short walk along the dirt access road brings you back to the trailhead parking. Though the mileage and elevation gain are modest, this can be a long day thanks to the challenging off-trail navigation in the first mile or so.

"The Citadel"–Hagar Mountain Traverse

Class 3+ – 8 miles – 3,400' elevation gain

This is a good, challenging day that strong hikers will love. The steep hills at the start will test your fitness, while the scrambles up "The Citadel" and Hagar Mountain will shift the focus to route-finding and climbing.

From the trailhead, work your way into Dry Gulch toward Fortress saddle between "The Citadel" (technically unnamed on maps) and UN 12,671. Fortress saddle is 2.5 miles from the trailhead and is reached by following the Dry Gulch Road until it becomes a trail. That trail soon disappears, and the rest of the day will be off-trail. Follow the second creek/drainage north to gain the steep slopes to the saddle. The jagged spire of "The Citadel" looks daunting from here, but it does have a weakness.

After reaching Fortress saddle, the steepness continues. Follow it another 0.5 mile (and 800 tough vertical feet) and pass under the summit block on the south side. There are a few Class 4 rock gullies here that access the east summit of "The Citadel"; these are optional. At mile 3.0 before the ridge drops toward Hagar Mountain, a sandy, loose gully offers access to a gap between the twin summits (both are nearly the same elevation, 13,294 feet, though the west summit is the "official" one). Class 3+ scrambles will gain access to both summits. The vertical drop off the north side of the tiny saddle between the two is breathtaking.

Once "The Citadel" is scaled, continue southwest to Hagar Mountain. Staying below the ridge on the south side is a good start, even if it's a little loose and sandy. Eventually, the Class 3 ridge to Hagar develops. It is 0.6 mile to the top. Choose to traverse a bit below the ridge for easier, Class 2+ terrain, or stay on the ridge for thrilling Class 3+ (possibly Class 4) scrambling, including a few "mini" knife-edges. Reach Hagar Mountain's east summit (the higher of the two) at 13,220 feet and 3.6 miles in. Downclimb the last bit of Class 3 terrain for the day to reach Hagar's 13,195-foot west summit and continue down Hagar's south slopes. Descend back into Dry Gulch at the saddle between Hagar and the north shoulder of "Golden Bear," staying on the north side of the basin as long as possible (the footing is solid along these slopes). Bypass a small lake, then continue, eventually picking a spot you like on the slopes and returning to the valley floor.

For an even bigger day, rather than descend into Dry Gulch, carry on south from the saddle to "Golden Bear Peak," 1.1 miles and 400 vertical feet away, then descend 3.0 miles down Loveland Ski Area's slopes to Chair 8 and back to I-70 and the trailhead.

Author's note: A formal memorial to the crash victims is at mile marker 217 near a large digital sign on westbound I-70. There is a pulloff to park as well. The memorial has the names of the victims and a small, white cross.

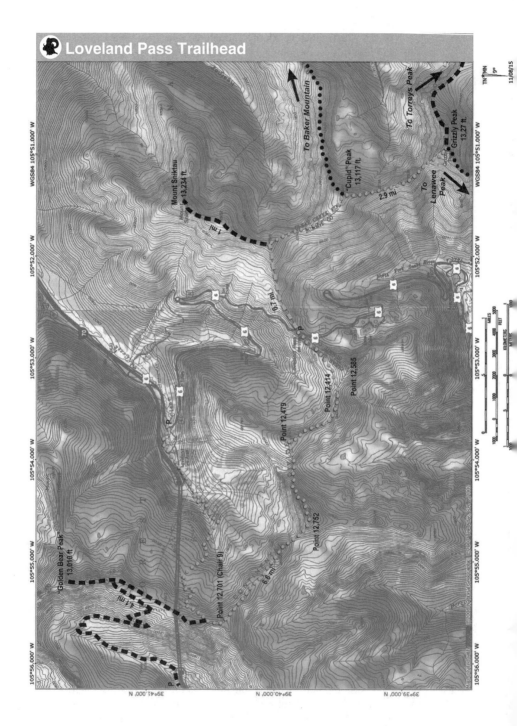

Loveland Pass Trailhead

Loveland Pass Trailhead (11,990')

The minute you step out of your car at Loveland Pass, you'll already have postcard-perfect views. The drive to the top of this thrilling paved pass is an adventure in itself. As for the hiking, heading up to the east grants access to several 13,000-foot peaks. Westward presents an often-overlooked traverse along the Continental Divide above the Loveland Ski Area. A classic traverse from Loveland Pass to Loveland Tunnel West can add in "Golden Bear Peak" without too much trouble—both the navigation and the parking set up nicely for this point-to-point.

PEAKS

- Mount Sniktau: 13,234'
- "Cupid" Peak: 13,117'
- Grizzly Peak: 13,427'
- Baker Mountain: 12,448' (see page 56)
- "Golden Bear Peak": 13,010'
- Mount Trelease: 12,477'
- Lenawee Peak: 13,204'
- (from Arapahoe Basin Ski Area)
- Continental Divide points (Loveland Ski Area, highest point: Point 12,752)

Wilderness Area and Range

Arapaho National Forest, Front Range

Trailhead Distance from I-70

4.2 miles

Driving Directions

Take Exit 216 to US 6 toward Loveland Pass. Coming westbound, go left off the exit, under the bridge, and then right at the split. Eastbound, go right off the exit. You'll pass the Loveland Ski Area (and point-to-point parking) and proceed up a series of steep, somewhat exposed paved switchbacks to the summit. Any car can make it to the trailhead parking on the top at 11,990 feet, though be aware of weather conditions . . . snow can come at any time. There is ample parking on the left (east) side of the road in a developed parking lot.

If you are parking at the Loveland Ski Area for the point-to-point along the Continental Divide, note that you cannot park in the main ski parking lot. Loveland has reserved a small portion left of the entrance gate for parking three or four vehicles in the summer, and there is no parking allowed along Loveland Pass after this. However, just before the entrance to Loveland, there is parking in a pulloff on the left (south) side of the road. It's down an abrupt dirt hill, but there is plenty of space to park.

Note: Loveland Ski Area has two parking sections: the Loveland Ski Area and Loveland Basin. If you go the wrong way off the exits, you could end up at Loveland Basin (which is a small bunny hill that is east of a more prominent main ski hill). Don't confuse the two—you want to park near Loveland Ski Area, not the basin.

Vehicle Recommendations	Any vehicle can make it up the paved pass in good conditions. When snow and ice are on the pass, check with the Colorado Department of Transportation (CDOT) for road conditions, as Loveland Pass does close from time to time when there are storms.
Fees/Camping	There are no fees to camp or hike here. If you are car camping, there is a small camping area at Pass Lake, 0.5 mile over the south side of the pass.
Dog Regulations	Dogs are allowed under voice control or on leash.
Summary	The big peaks off the east side of the pass are well known—they are often hiked year-round thanks to the wind-swept ridges that stay relatively avalanche-free in the winter. These mountains offer a great workout since they begin uphill right out of the parking lot but never have any technical terrain, excepting the small scramble up Grizzly Peak (Class 2+).

What many people miss is the excellent circuit off the west side of the pass, which traverses high above the Loveland Ski Area until it ultimately merges with it. A series of high 12,000-plus-foot points culminates with Point 12,752, which will feel very much like a "real" mountain when you chug up its steep slopes. A summer descent down Loveland Ski Area is interesting—keep your eyes open for lost GoPros, gloves, and other goodies. Swinging over to "Golden Bear Peak," 13,010 feet, then down to Loveland Tunnel West parking is a good, all-day point-to-point that isn't too demanding and never gets technical. |

Primary Routes

16. ❂ Mount Sniktau (13,284') to Grizzly Peak (13,427')

Round-Trip Distance	7.1 miles
Class	2+
Difficulty	5/10
Hiking Time	5–7 hours
Total Elevation Gain	3,860'
Terrain	Rolling hills with no established trails that can get steep at times; the traverse to Grizzly has some easy Class 2 scrambling on good rock.
Best Time to Climb	June–October, though this route is a good option year-round

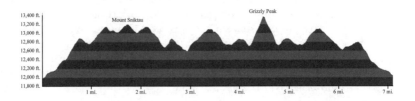

This hike wastes no time getting started with the elevation gain. You'll go more than 1,000 vertical feet in the first 0.7 mile, though thankfully it's along a wide ridge with good footing (and plenty of hiker's trails). Once at the top of this initial hill, there are options to head north to Mount Sniktau—and the rarely climbed Baker Mountain—or south toward Grizzly Peak (also known as Grizzly Peak D because it's the fourth-highest of Colorado's named "Grizzly" peaks). Sniktau as a direct out-and-back is a fun, quick summit hike of 3.0 miles that strong hikers can knock out in a few hours. Read the "Additional Routes" section on page 87 about connecting to Baker Mountain and Grays/Torreys Peaks as point-to-points.

0.0 From the eastside parking lot, head up along an obvious ridge that will connect you with the main north–south ridge. Note that you'll be hiking right on the Continental Divide. It's only if you turn north toward Sniktau that you leave the divide proper. Hiking here will be steep, and many people feel the altitude right away—the hike starts at 11,990 feet.

0.7 After a good warm-up, the access ridge joins the main ridge. Views are already incredible, especially of the castlelike towers of "The Citadel" to the north. Heading south right away at this point is a common route—feel free to head out this way if you'd like to eschew Mount Sniktau. Otherwise, carry on north (left) toward Sniktau.

1.3 Point 13,152 is a prominent bump that may initially be mistaken for Mount Sniktau—until you're standing atop it. Sniktau is just a short ways ahead along continued Class 2 terrain. A spectacular snowfield and cornice often populates the eastern side of this ridge year-round.

1.7 Sniktau's summit. Soak it in, then turn around and return to the connecting access ridge to the parking area.

2.6 Back at the junction of ridges, now it's time to head south (or . . . back to the parking lot if you've had your fill).

3.3 After dipping down to 12,608 feet, climb to UN 13,417, which also (unfortunately) goes by the mawkish moniker "Cupid" peak. While this author and the U.S. Geological Survey (USGS) do not recognize this name, enough local hikers do that it should be mentioned. Despite the name, it's a worthy summit.

Note: The ridge that runs east of "Cupid" heads down to Baker Mountain and eventually Grizzly Gulch. This is a neat point-to-point, especially starting from Grizzly Gulch. See "Additional Routes" on page 87 for more details.

Continue along the ridge, where the terrain upgrades to light scrambling. Faint trails come and go along the ridge.

4.1 At Point 12,936, Grizzly is in striking distance, but there is the matter of a quick downclimb to a narrow saddle at 12,630 feet before heading up. The northwest ridge of Grizzly looks tougher than it actually is—all Class 2+ scrambling on good rock. From the saddle it's 0.3 mile and 800 vertical feet (!) to the top.

4.5 The windswept summit of Grizzly Peak. The connecting ridge to Torreys is quite enticing from here—and it's possible as a nice point-to-point to Stevens Gulch or a very long out-and-back day. Don't worry though; heading back the way you came dials up a few hundred more feet of elevation gain, so

Walking the ridgelines toward Loveland Ski Area

you'll get a workout on the way home. Return back along the ridge, occasionally skirting high points on the ridge on the west (left) side.

6.4 After rolling along the ridge, you'll be back at the access ridge with Loveland Pass twisting through the mountains below you. Set a course dead west and head for the parking lot.

7.1 Finish.

Notes Approaching on westbound I-70, Mount Sniktau's enormous dome looms high on the south side of the highway—impress all your friends by pointing it out. I don't know why the peaks in this area get labeled with such goofy names, but unlike the informally named "Cupid," Sniktau is an officially recognized USGS title. Edwin Patterson, a journalist in the area in the 1860s, adopted the nickname Sniktau by reversing his colleague's last name: W. F. Watkins. And because Patterson had friends in all the right places, the mountain bears his name today.

A further footnote about Mount Sniktau: It was planned to be turned into a bona fide ski mountain when Denver was awarded the 1976 Olympics. That changed once Vail was sussed out to be a superior locale; then the whole thing was scrapped when Colorado voters rejected the funding needed to bring the winter games to the state. Eventually, the whole operation moved to Innsbruck, Austria, and somewhere in the ether, the ghost of Edwin Patterson wept.

17. ✪ Continental Divide Point-to-Point Tour–Highest Point (12,752')

Round-Trip Distance	6.6 miles
Class	2
Difficulty	4/10
Hiking Time	5–7 hours
Total Elevation Gain	2,200'
Terrain	Rolling ridges with informal trails and descent down snowcat roads in Loveland Ski Area.
Best Time to Climb	June–October

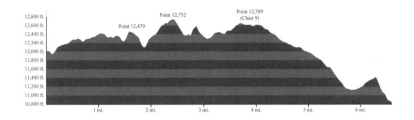

Overview Winter backcountry skiers know this ridge well, but it tends to get overlooked by many hikers in the summer. What starts out as a rather tame, pleasant amble across broad ridges evolves into something burlier, though the route never surpasses Class 2 in difficulty. It does have some steep ups and downs though. Dropping down from Point 12,479 then climbing up to Point 12,752 is the crux of the adventure, as the terrain between the two looks sketchy until you're actually in it. After that, cruise into Loveland Ski Area, where out-of-season Chair 9, 12,700 feet, offers a snowcat road back down to the base of Loveland Pass. Adding on "Golden Bear Peak" (13,010') will be easy for strong hikers. In this case, wrapping up your point-to-point at the Loveland Tunnel West parking area (see page 89) is an excellent option and a better walk-off than descending the sometimes-steep slopes of the ski area (or retracing your steps to Chair 9).

Mile/Route **0.0** Carefully cross Loveland Pass and head west along some established but unmarked trails. The first mile of this hike is a nice warm-up with only moderate elevation gains. The entirety of the route is laid out before you.
0.6 Point 12,585 is above on your left side—most people skip this point and aim for the saddle between it and 12,414 where the trail goes. Continue west.
1.4 Point 12,479 can be ascended or bypassed on the west side for a more direct path. The saddle between it and Point 12,752 looks like it might present some difficulty. However, if you stay right on the top of the ridge, a path wends down through rock outcrops to the saddle. Footing can be a little loose, but it's not exposed or tougher than Class 2.

Enjoying the western views from the ridgeline

1.7 At 12,100 feet, the steep, steady challenge of Point 12,752 awaits . . . 600 vertical feet in 0.5 mile to the top!

2.2 The flat summit of Point 12,752. If you don't tack on the optional summit of "Golden Bear Peak," this is your highest point of the day. At this point, you safely bail down into Loveland Ski Area almost anywhere. Views are great to the west, but don't forget to look back toward Loveland Pass to see how far you've come. Descend northwest off the peak and roll the rest of the ridge toward Chair 9. You'll go over a few small bumps and reach a low point of 12,400 feet before the last walk up to Chair 9.

3.9 The last high point at Chair 9. There are snowcat roads and clear visual lines down to the ski lodge and the parking area. Take whichever way down suits you best—either the grassy slopes or along the snowcat road.

6.6 Pass the lodge and main ski area parking lot to your vehicle waiting below. Mileage may vary depending on how directly you descend.

Notes The Loveland West Tunnel route is an 8.2-mile point-to-point. It adds 730 feet of vertical elevation and is a worthwhile traverse. It's much easier to do this route when the horseshoe access road for Loveland Tunnel West parking allows you to quickly get back on I-70 E (see page 90 for details on this and give CDOT a ring at 303-757-9011 to see if it's open). If it's not, you'll have to drive all the way down the west side of the pass and get on eastbound I-70 in Silverthorne, then drive back up to Loveland Pass to start your like. Either way, once the cars are figured out, this is an exciting tour. Very strong hikers can include Coon Hill's east ridge for a crowning summit at the end of a long day.

Additional Routes

Loveland Pass–Stevens Gulch Point-to-Point

Class 2 – 8.2 miles – 4,300' elevation gain

This time, one vehicle parks at Stevens Gulch (see page 55) and the second at Loveland Pass. Head over to Grizzly (2.8 miles as a direct hike from the parking, over "Cupid") then drop east then southeast to Torreys Peak's Class 2+ east ridge. It's 1.8 miles from Grizzly to Torreys. After reaching the fourteener by the novel route, head down the trails to Stevens Gulch parking. Add on Grays if it seems fitting.

If you're incredibly fit, acclimated, and have the time to set up two cars, Loveland Pass to Guenella Pass adds on Grays, Mount Edwards, Argentine Peak, and Square Top Mountain after Torreys Peak—13.6 miles and nearly 7,500 vertical feet of elevation gain. An awesome huge day that may require a little training to get up the endurance, but you'll earn some bragging rights to go along with those four thirteeners and two fourteeners.

"Cupid" Peak (13,117') to Baker Mountain (12,448') Point-to-Point

Class 2 – 4.8 miles – 1,810' elevation gain

For this unusual route, one vehicle is parked at Grizzly Gulch (see page 55) and the other at Loveland Pass. Head up to "Cupid" Peak, then head down the east ridge to the seldom visited Baker Mountain (which looks like a mere bump from above). It's 3.3 miles to Baker, then follow an open avalanche path through the woods down to Grizzly Gulch road and walk out east to your awaiting vehicle. Starting at Grizzly and ending at Loveland Pass may be an even better adventure.

Extra Credit

Lenawee Peak (13,204') (from Arapahoe Basin)

Class 3 – 7 miles – 2,420' elevation gain

The ridge connecting Lenawee and Grizzly Peaks is either hard Class 3 or legit Class 4, so it's outside the "rules" of this guide. However, Lenawee Peak can be a fun day from Arapahoe Ski Basin parking. Drive up and over Loveland Pass and hit the A-Basin parking lot at 8.0 miles on the left side of the road. This is on national forest land, so you are free to hike up. Hike the ski area, first up along the Black Mountain Express then under the Norway or Lenawee Lifts. This brings you to a high saddle at 12,360 feet, 2.1 miles up. Head east along Lenawee Ridge for some fun Class 3 scrambling and routefinding to Lenawee's summit at 3.8 miles. Return the way you came.

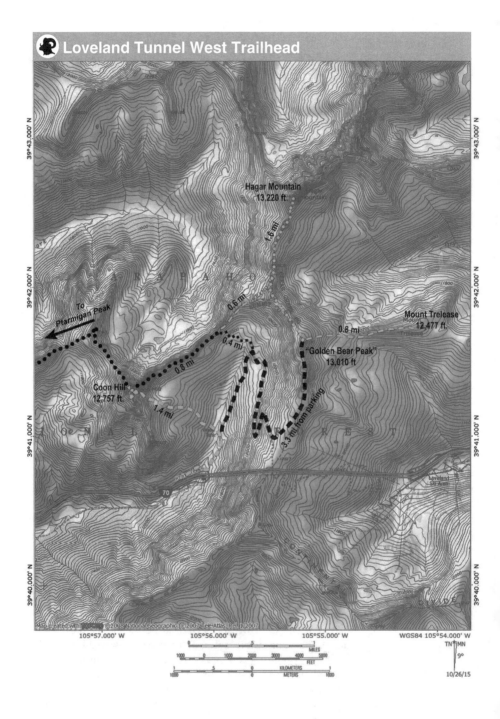

Loveland Tunnel West Trailhead

Hagar Mountain
13,220 ft.

1.6 mi

0.6 mi

To
Ptarmigan Peak

Mount Trelease
12,477 ft.

0.8 mi

0.4 mi

"Golden Bear Peak"
13,010 ft

0.8 mi

Coon Hill
12,757 ft.

1.4 mi

3.3 mi from parking

70

Loveland
Ski Area

39°43.000' N

39°42.000' N

39°41.000' N

39°40.000' N

105°57.000' W   105°56.000' W   105°55.000' W   WGS84 105°54.000' W

TN MN
9°

10/26/15

Map created with TOPO! ©2018 National Geographic. ©2002 Tele Atlas, Rel 01/2007

MILES
FEET
KILOMETERS
METERS

XI. Loveland Tunnel West Trailhead (10,120')

As far as trailheads go, this one isn't very charming. It's not off an official exit, it has no fancy signs, and the parking area is a gravel lot 40 feet from the roaring highway. But all is not what it seems! This overlooked trailhead is the gateway to fantastic summits, notably a collection of unnamed peaks in the seldom-visited Williams Fork Range.

PEAKS

- "Golden Bear Peak": 13,010'
- Coon Hill: 12,757'
- Hagar Mountain: 13,220' (also see page 72)
- Ptarmigan Peak: 12,498' (see page 100)
- Mount Trelease: 12,477' (also see page 72)

Wilderness Area and Range

White River National Forest, Ptarmigan Peak Wilderness, Front Range, Williams Fork Range

Trailhead Distance from I-70

Directly off I-70

Driving Directions

Loveland Tunnel West Trailhead is an easy one to miss—but oddly, also an easy one to find. It is located on the immediate exit (no number) upon exit of westbound I-70 on through the Eisenhower–Johnson Memorial Tunnel, also known as the Loveland Tunnel.

I-70 W: Go through the Eisenhower–Johnson Memorial Tunnel. Get in the right lane. As soon as you exit the tunnel, take a quick right at the exit marked TRUCK BRAKE CHECK—believe it or not, this is the trailhead! Drive about 200 feet west and park in a scrappy lot on the right with a makeshift TRAILHEAD PARKING sign. You can also park away near the concrete barriers farther south. Just be sure not to park near the Colorado Department of Transportation (CDOT) buildings east of this exit.

I-70 E: The easiest way to park is to go through the Eisenhower–Johnson Memorial Tunnel (temporarily bypassing your trailhead) and take Exit 216 toward Loveland Ski Area. Take a left off this exit, then another left to loop around and get back on I-70 W. Go back through the tunnel and follow the directions above for I-70 W.

Note that this road is directly next to the highway with no barriers. Be quadruply vigilant when taking dogs along—make sure they are securely leashed when exiting your vehicle.

Special note: You can sometimes return to I-70 via the paved horseshoe road around the east side of the tunnel, though CDOT often closes this road for public access (call ahead: 303-757-9011). Be warned, though, that the merge onto the highway eastbound (just in front of the tunnel)

can be tricky, especially in thick traffic. When it is closed, those returning eastbound to Denver/Boulder will have to drive down the pass to Exit 205 in Dillon and turn around.

Vehicle Recommendations   Any working vehicle can make this trailhead—it's just off the road in a paved/gravel lot.

Fees/Camping   There are no fees to hike here. Camping is allowed in White River National Forest. Overnight car camping is technically allowed but not suggested, since you're all of 40 feet away from the highway. Pitching a tent about 0.25 mile from the trailhead is actually quite nice.

Dog Regulations   Dogs on leash are allowed in White River National Forest and the Ptarmigan Wilderness.

Summary   Loveland West's ugly facade quickly gives way to one of the most spectacular wildflower basins in Colorado. Only a few hundred feet from the busy parking area, Straight Creek Basin explodes with color from late spring to late summer. A well-established trail heads up to "Golden Bear Peak," the high point of the Loveland Ski Area. From there, Hagar Mountain, Coon Hill, Mount Trelease, and the unnamed peaks of Loveland Ski Area are all nearby. There are also some fun combos to link together, such as the brief but exciting Class 3 ridge of Coon Hill and an epic 13.4-mile traverse along the Williams Fork Mountains.

There's a lot of wildlife in this basin, so it's a good idea to keep your pups leashed up (especially below treeline). Views from these peaks are special; you can see far west to the Gore and Sawatch Ranges and east all the way to Denver on a clear day. Crowds are low and the scenic rewards are quickly reaped. "Golden Bear Peak" is the gem of this basin and has well-used, well-graded trail to its ridgeline. Check out the special options section for great point-to-point options as well.

Primary Routes

18. Coon Hill Direct (12,757')

Round-Trip Distance	2.8 miles
Class	2
Difficulty	5/10
Hiking Time	3–4 hours
Total Elevation Gain	1,622'
Terrain	Brief on-trail path leads to grassy, steep-but-stable off-trail slopes. Poles are a very good idea.
Best Time to Climb	Mid-May–early October

Overview   This is the closest thing to a standard route on Coon Hill. Brief, burly, and beautiful, the slope to the summit starts as a series of small hills

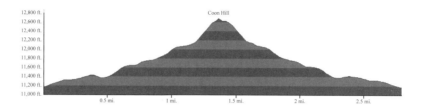

then culminates in a 500-vertical-foot push to the top. While it is steep, there's no scary exposure, and the summit is a flat, welcoming haven above the highway.

For a longer day, check out the "Golden Bear"–Coon Hill traverse.

Mile/Route 0.0 From the parking area, head east along a brief service road (not the horseshoe road). You will pass the tunnel facility buildings on your right. Carry on to the end of this paved section. If it's wildflower season, be prepared for a dazzling show, highlighted by Indian paintbrush and columbine. 0.3 The pavement ends. Continue along the wide, well-worn trail into the basin. Already, I-70 is slipping away and the impressive alpine beauty of the basin is revealing itself.

Looking into Straight Creek Basin from the high shoulder of Coon Hill

0.5 Split from the main trail. The rest of your hike will be easy-to-navigate off-trail terrain. There's a simple creek crossing after diverging from the path. Coon Hill's true summit, hidden from the road, will slowly come into view and the access slope looks *steep*. Carry on up the slopes, aiming for southeast slope in the middle of the peak. Hike around or scramble up the little rock outcrops.

1.2 You are at the base of the summit slope at 12,260 feet—get ready to grind. It's less than a quarter mile to the summit, but the grade is a stiff 25- to 33-degree slope over 500 vertical feet. Thankfully, the footing is relatively solid grass and rock. Start up near the rock outcrops on the left, then begin switchbacking up. Just before the summit, it's helpful to gain the east ridge rather than plow directly up.

1.4 Coon Hill's summit, 12,757 feet! The flat, broad summit is perfect for a scenic lunch. The cars streaming down the highway will be dwarfed by the Tenmile Range and Gore Range peaks to the west. Descend the same way you came. Hiking poles are strongly encouraged for the descent. The line of site to the low point in the basin makes this an easy path to navigate.

2.8 Finish.

Variation

East Ridge

Class 3 – 3.8 miles

This fun scramble is an excellent option with a bit of unexpectedly challenging route-finding near the summit. Start the same way as Coon Hill Direct, but rather than turning off the trail at 0.5 mile, continue on the well-worn trail up to "Golden Bear." At 1.2 miles, the trail makes a sharp switchback. Exit the trail here and continue north 0.4 mile toward the ridge between Coon and the 12,855-foot shoulder of "Golden Bear." A faint climber's trail appears out of the ether, then switchbacks up to a low point in the ridge at 1.6 miles.

Cruise west along pleasant, easygoing terrain until you reach mile 2.2 at 12,370 feet. The last 0.2 mile of this ridge requires some genuine Class 3 scrambling. The first short section is navigated by staying below the ridge on the east side, where jutting rocks make the off-camber slopes a little tricky. Arriving at a small saddle, the scrambling gets much more enjoyable. Stay on the south side, scrambling along a tight gully until you regain the ridge. White and gray rock eases up and brings you the top at 2.4 miles. Return via the Coon Hill Direct slopes.

19. ✪ "Golden Bear Peak" (13,010')

Round-Trip Distance	6.7 miles
Class	2
Difficulty	3/10
Hiking Time	3–4 hours
Total Elevation Gain	2,058'
Terrain	Gradual, enjoyable Class 2 trail to ridgeline. Easy, off-trail Class 2 ridge walk to summit.
Best Time to Climb	Mid-May–early October

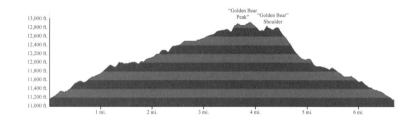

Overview   This mountainoid is not officially named, but it is an officially ranked thirteener (634 of 637). This is one of the very best pure Class 2 hikes off I-70 and a great intro to high-altitude hiking for newer hikers. The trail is easy to follow and maintains a kindly, gradual grade. It may also be the only summit that affords views of both the east and west entrances of the Eisenhower–Johnson Tunnel. A great hike as an out-and-back, it's an equally fun circuit to loop down to the low point of the Coon–"Golden Bear" north shoulder ridge (6.1 miles, 2,200' elevation gain, Class 2). "Golden Bear" is also the launching point for Hagar Mountain and the "Golden Bear"–Coon traverse.

Mile/Route   **0.0**   From the parking area, head east along a brief service road (not the horseshoe road). You will pass the tunnel facility buildings on your right. Carry on to the end of this paved section—this is the same start as Coon Hill Direct, so you'll be treated to the same glorious wildflower show.
0.3   The pavement ends, and the trail continues north into the basin. Continue along the dirt trail.
1.9   Continue to follow the trail as it hits a big switchback and heads south. If you choose to do the loop option mentioned in the overview, this is where you will reconnect with the main trail. Soak in the morning sun lighting up the western peaks as you climb along the trail.
2.4   After two more switchbacks, there's something of a trail split. Since you need to gain the ridge and head north, split off here and gain the ridge. You'll see a few posts and fence sections on the ridge, courtesy of Loveland Ski Area. Note that come winter, you can take a snowcat and hike to "Golden Bear Peak" at Loveland Ski Area by following the ridge; it's in bounds!

Coon Hill as seen from the shoulder of "Golden Bear Peak"

2.6 Gain the ridge and continue north. Optional easy scrambles await at the presummits.

3.3 The summit of "Golden Bear." There's lots to see from here. Hagar Mountain and the west side of "The Citadel" are especially impressive. Even Coon Hill looks more mountainous from this vantage. Descend the way you came or continue north a little over 0.3 mile to the north shoulder of "Golden Bear." Follow the ridge west to the low point in the ridge where a visible climber's trail joins the ridge. Follow it back to the main trail (easy off-trail with good sight lines).

6.7 End back at the parking area.

20. ✪ Hagar Mountain (13,220') via "Golden Bear Peak"

Round-Trip Distance	7.8 miles
Class	3
Difficulty	6/10
Hiking Time	5–7 hours
Total Elevation Gain	2,868'
Terrain	Steady, easy Class 2 to "Golden Bear Peak," then rolling terrain to steep hike to Hagar's west subsummit. A short, Class 3 scramble on solid rock. Great hero shots if one person waits on the subsummit.
Best Time to Climb	Late May–early October

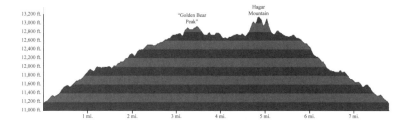

| | | | | Hagar Mountain | | | |
| | | | "Golden Bear" Peak" | | | | |

13,200 ft.
13,000 ft.
12,800 ft.
12,600 ft.
12,400 ft.
12,200 ft.
12,000 ft.
11,800 ft.
11,600 ft.
11,400 ft.
11,200 ft.
11,000 ft.

1 mi.   2 mi.   3 mi.   4 mi.   5 mi.   6 mi.   7 mi.

Overview Another absolute classic out of the Loveland West Trailhead. Start with "Golden Bear Peak," a fine hike in its own right, and then carry on north. Hagar looks especially inviting from the ridgeline past "Golden Bear." A steep push leads to the subsummit—the perfect place to park your dogs with a friend while you snag the summit. There are great photo ops if one person waits on the subsummit—then take turns. The final scramble is solid, fun, and slightly exposed. On the way back, dip below the north shoulder of "Golden Bear" and make a lovely loop back to the parking area.

A victory wave from the summit of Hagar Mountain

0.0 From the parking lot, follow the "Golden Bear" route to its summit at 13,010 feet and 3.3 miles. Now that you're warmed up, it's time to work.

3.3 The summit of "Golden Bear." Continue north along the ridge. Easy, Class 2 downclimbs eventually connect to Coon Hill's east ridge at 3.9 miles.

4.0 Continue north, then northeast, as you follow the natural contours of the ridge toward Hagar. It cuts a mighty profile from the ridge.

4.5 At a small dip at 12,890 feet, you'll be at the start of the steep slope leading to Hagar's west subsummit. Take a moment to gaze east into the Dry Gulch Basin, where Mount Bethel anchors the eastern fringe of Dry Gulch's peaks.

4.7 The 0.2 mile of steep climbing isn't nearly as bad as it looks from below—it's just over 200 total vertical feet. After cresting the high ridge around 13,100 feet, you'll have a clear view of Hagar's true summit block. An easy down-climb into a saddle serves as a prelude for the final scramble. The 100 vertical feet of rock have slightly easier lines on the south (right) side, and sticking to the middle of the ridge is solid, with a few simple but thrilling moves.

4.9 Hagar's summit isn't big, but there's enough room for three or four people. The goal now is to get back to the east ridge of Coon Hill. Because you can skirt the final peaks on the north side, you can avoid tacking on needless elevation on the way back.

5.4 About this time, shear off the ridge and make a direct path to Coon Hill's east ridge. Keep your eyes open for abandoned mines along the way.

6.0 Around 6 miles, you'll be on Coon Hill's east ridge. Continue west on the accommodating ridge toward the low point. A visible climber's trail switchbacks into Straight Creek Basin.

6.2 Take the faint but noticeable climber's trail in the basin. It disappears through a brief swampy section, but the course is visually simple. If for some reason you lose the trail, following the low point of the basin where the creek flows will eventually get you back to the main path.

6.8 Regain the main trail and head home. By all means, stop and smell the flowers along the way.

7.8 Finish.

Additional Routes

There is a wealth of excellent ways to link up mountains in this area, including some epic point-to-point options. Here are a few to consider.

"Golden Bear"–Hagar–Coon Hill via East Ridge

Class 3 – 8.3 miles – 3,742' elevation gain

Follow the Hagar route, except tack on Coon Hill's Class 3 east ridge finish. Don't let the modest mileage fool you; this is a demanding circuit.

"Golden Bear"–Hagar–"The Citadel" Point-to-Point

Class 3 – 9–10 miles – 4,000' elevation gain

Again follow Hagar's route and continue northeast to the towering twin mountainoid summits of "The Citadel" (see Herman Gulch, page 62). The ridge connecting Hagar and "The Citadel" is rarely visited and makes for a unique scramble. As a point-to-point, descend east to Fortress saddle, then either drop down into Dry Gulch (more direct, more bushwhacking) or Herman Gulch (short off-trail to longer, but easy-to-follow, well-established trail). I'd suggest the Herman Gulch exit, as the bushwhacking and steepness of Dry Gulch can be annoying at the end of a long day.

If you'd like a lighter version of this day ending in Dry Gulch, consider going from "Golden Bear" to Mount Trelease (12,477'). Trelease is 0.8 mile east from the summit of "Golden Bear" and another 2.2 miles of bushwhacking and trail to the Dry Gulch parking area.

"Golden Bear"–Loveland Ski Area or Loveland Pass

Class 2 – 8 miles (Loveland Pass) – 3,400' elevation gain

This point-to-point is a cloud walker's delight. Start with "Golden Bear" (or eschew it for a direct line to Loveland Ski Area). Reverse the Loveland Ski Area ridge circuit (see page 80) all the way to Loveland Pass. There are a few stiff up and downs, but fit hikers will really enjoy the prolonged time above treeline. Finishing with a descent through Loveland Ski Area (6- to 7-mile day) is perfectly acceptable—just park at the base of the ski area rather than the summit of Loveland Pass.

The Coon Clamber

Class 3 – 2.2 miles – 1,900' elevation gain

This route is even more direct than the Coon Hill Direct. If hands-and-knees power scrambling is your thing, this Class 3 route (with lots of Class 4 and 5 options) is for you. It wastes no time, grinding directly up the south shoulder of Coon Hill. The rock is good, though finding the easiest line can be some work. It's barely over a mile to the summit, but it will be a hard-earned victory.

Special Route

✪ Coon Hill (12,757') to Ptarmigan Peak (12,498')

Class 2 – 12.9 miles – 3,900' elevation gain *(see maps on pages 88 and 100)*

The ultimate I-70 tour. This point-to-point starts at Coon Hill and ends at the Ptarmigan Peak Trailhead parking in Silverthorne (see page 101 for driving directions to this trailhead). Strong hikers will delight in this isolated tour of the Williams Fork Mountains, stepping foot where few dare to go (even though it's only about an hour from Denver). The burly grind up Coon Hill is just the start. Follow the long, rolling west ridge along a series of unnamed but distinct peaks, including UN 12,411, UN 12,346, UN 12,429, UN 12,221, and UN 12,212. A quick descent to Ptarmigan Pass wraps up with an ascent up Ptarmigan Peak, 12,498 feet (and a 5.0-mile walk down).

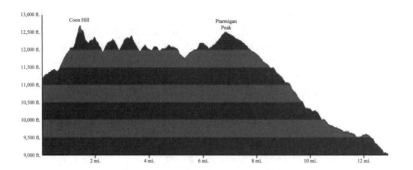

The constant up and down makes for a hearty day. Starting early is an absolute must, even for strong hikers. Besides the incredibly exposed, above-treeline terrain, the descent off Ptarmigan into Silverthorne can get broiling on a summer's day. This is the perfect big day for a cool autumn adventure. Expect to see plenty of wildlife in the peaks (if you're taking Fido, please keep him on leash and bring extra water).

Park one car at Coon Hill and another at Ptarmigan Peak Trailhead (see page 100 for details).

Mile/Route   **0.0** Start from the Loveland Tunnel West parking, and your warm-up (!) is Coon Hill. Have fun!

1.4 Coon Hill summit. This is highest point of your day. You'll gain about 3,800 feet of elevation but *lose* over 6,000 feet, so bring your hiking poles. The traverse follows the long ridge west to Ptarmigan Peak (looming very far away at the end of the chain). Start off by descending off the northwest ridge of Coon toward UN 12,411.

2.0 UN 12,411. From here, your adventure takes you west along the ridge until you reach Ptarmigan Pass, so the navigation is easy. This area is beautiful and unspoiled—you'll see what I mean when you arrive. The terrain for the rest of the day is Class 2, off-trail until the descent trail off Ptarmigan Peak.

2.9 UN 12,346. In 2015 this summit had a register with some quirky entries. If it were a foot lower, it would be UN 1-2-3-4-5. Coon Hill looks quite impressive from this unique vantage point.

3.5 UN 12,429.

4.1 UN 12,221, a summit that should be called Palindrome Peak.

5.4 After five summits, most people will skip UN 12,243 just to the south. However, if you do grab it, your end mileage will be about 13.1 miles—a half marathon!

Drop down to Ptarmigan Pass, where established trails and a weathered signpost offer the first evidence of human development. If your legs aren't burning at this point, the 720 vertical feet up to Ptarmigan Peak (the seventh summit of the day) may do the trick. Note the small, glimmering lake to the north (your right) as you ascend; it looks like there is a lake within the lake!

6.0 UN 12,212—the sixth summit of the day and the confusing cousin of UN 12,221.

6.8 The broad, flat summit of Ptarmigan Peak. Behold the Gore Range to the west! Lake Dillon to southwest! Faraway Coon Hill to the east! And Ute Peak to the north! Mentally prepare for a long, on-trail descent that rivals Longs Peak's famous walk out from the Keyhole. The descent from here is 3,500 feet and can get roasting hot on summer afternoons.

8.5 At a fork in the trail, there are two well-worn trails; both go to the trailhead. The right (north) trail is 2.6 miles and has more gentle switchbacks. The left trail is 2.4 miles, so 0.2 mile shorter, but is a little more direct and tougher on the knees. Either will work, but I recommend the longer fork because it's an easier trail.

12.3 At 9,300 feet, you'll emerge into the small neighborhood near where you parked your second vehicle, which may feel like eons ago at this point. Follow the dirt roads south and then west to the parking area that overlooks I-70.

12.9 Finish! Congratulations, you've completed one of Colorado's best hiking traverses. A seven-summit is nothing to sneeze at.

Looking at Hagar Mountain from the Hagar–"Golden Bear" saddle (see page 94)

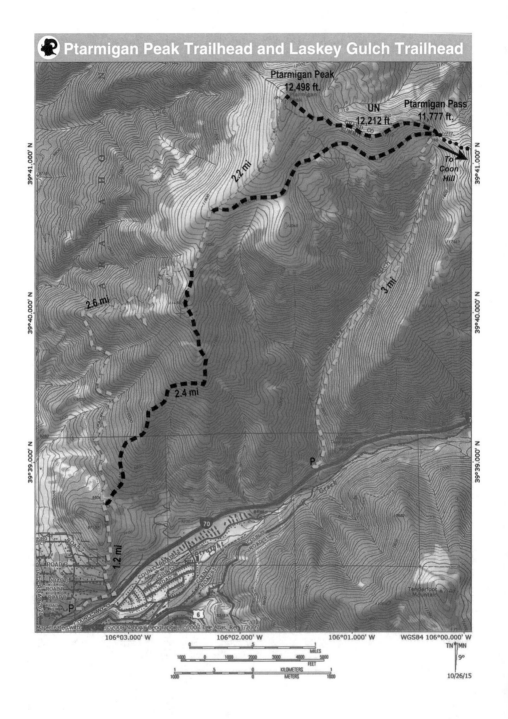

Ptarmigan Peak Trailhead and Laskey Gulch Trailhead

Ptarmigan Peak
12,498 ft.

UN
12,212 ft.

Ptarmigan Pass
11,777 ft.

To Coon Hill

2.2 mi

2.6 mi

3 mi

2.4 mi

P

1.2 mi

P

70

6

39°41,000' N

39°40,000' N

39°39,000' N

106°03,000' W   106°02,000' W   106°01,000' W   WGS84 106°00,000' W

TN MN

9°

MILES
FEET
KILOMETERS
METERS

Map created with TOPO! ©2008 National Geographic ©2004 Tele Atlas, Rel. 7/2007

10/26/15

XII.   Ptarmigan Peak Trailhead (8,990')
and Laskey Gulch Trailhead (9,500')

Despite a modest elevation of 12,498 feet, the standard route on Ptarmigan Peak covers more than 3,800 feet of elevation gain in a 12-mile round-trip. This is a good, full day out. The Class 1 trail makes it easy to daydream among the vanilla-scented pines. Above treeline, the views of Lake Dillon, the Tenmile Range, and the Gore Range are outstanding. Laskey Gulch is a hidden trailhead that offers a quiet, local's secret that goes to Ptarmigan Pass and, if you like, Ptarmigan Peak.

PEAKS

- Ptarmigan Peak: 12,498'
- UN 12,212: 12,212'

Wilderness Area and Range

Ptarmigan Peak Wilderness, White River National Forest, Williams Fork Mountains Range

Trailhead Distance from I-70

Ptarmigan Peak Trailhead: 1.5 miles

Laskey Gulch Trailhead: 100 feet

Driving Directions

Ptarmigan Peak Trailhead: Take Exit 205. Westbound, turn right onto CO 9 N at the end of the exit. Eastbound, turn left at the exit end to get on CO 9 N. Turn right onto Rainbow Road at a light in 0.2 mile. In about 250 feet, turn right onto Tanglewood Lane. In 0.2 mile, turn right onto Ptarmigan Trail. Parallel I-70 0.3 mile as Ptarmigan Trail turns to gravel. The parking area is on the right and overlooks the highway. Note that parking above this official trailhead is not allowed because the road enters a private community. The trail begins across the street to the north at a signed trail.

Laskey Gulch Trailhead: This trailhead (if you can call it that) is only accessible from I-70 westbound. From the Eisenhower–Johnson Memorial Tunnel, reset your odometer. At mile 5.2, after the second prominent runaway truck ramp, get into the right, breakdown lane (for goodness sake, please don't park in the runaway truck ramp). About 100 feet past the runaway truck ramp is a small dirt pulloff and parking area for four or five vehicles. Be careful when you return onto the highway.

Vehicle Recommendations

Passenger cars can access these trailheads.

Fees/Camping

There are no fees to hike or camp in this area. Note that both these trailheads are terrible car camping destinations. The town of Dillon has several reasonably priced but busy campgrounds nearby at Lake Dillon. For more info, visit its website at townofdillon.com or call 970-468-2403.

Dog Regulations Dogs are allowed on leash. Be quadruply vigilant at Laskey Gulch and leash those pups as soon as they are out of the vehicle. I-70 is literally roaring by 20 feet away.

Summary The 13,175-acre Ptarmigan Peak Wilderness is little known beyond Silverthorne area locals. Established in 1993, it offers access to the equally anonymous Williams Fork Range, a subsection within the western reaches of the Front Range. (There is actually a second Williams Fork mountain range in Moffat County.) Ptarmigan Peak's generous, grassy dome is the only major summit is this area, though the humble UN 12,212 qualifies as a nice little side peak. The trails out of the Ptarmigan Peak Trailhead are Class 1, but don't let that fool you. This is a big day with 3,800 feet of gain. Laskey Gulch is a tricky trailhead to access. It is a small pulloff immediately off I-70 westbound. The Laskey Gulch Trail is a hidden gem that heads up to Ptarmigan Pass.

The Ptarmigan Peak Trailhead is also the western terminus of the epic Coon Hill–Ptarmigan Peak traverse (see page 97 for details).

Primary Routes

21. ✪ Ptarmigan Peak (12,498') Loop

Round-Trip Distance	12 miles
Class	1
Difficulty	5/10
Hiking Time	5–8 hours
Total Elevation Gain	3,830'
Terrain	Smooth, well-maintained trail.
Best Time to Climb	April–November. Winter ascents are fun too, but a huge day if you're on snowshoes.

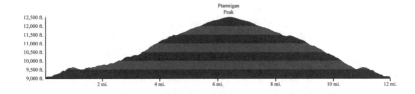

Overview This loop uses both of the primary access trails to gain the summit and switch up the scenery a little bit on the way down. Photography buffs should start before dawn to catch the morning sun shining west on the Tenmile and Gore Ranges to the west. Lodgepole pine and Engelmann spruce have been hard hit by beetle kill. You will walk among the ghosts of thousands of trees in lower forests. There's nothing extreme about this route, which is part of the charm. It's a wonderful place to enjoy a good conversation while getting a great workout. It has a local reputation as being a solid training ground for the fourteeners, as well as an excellent all-day hike, though it can get quite hot in the summer months.

The author poses with his family on the picture-perfect summit of Ptarmigan Peak.

Mile/Route **0.0** Across the street from the trailhead is a large Ptarmigan Peak info kiosk. Take this short trail through a small patch of woods and emerge . . . back in the neighborhood? Yes! Hike on the main dirt road north, ignoring an unmarked four-wheel-drive road cutting off to the right (east). At 0.4 mile, a signed trail for Ptarmigan Peak appears. Take it and head up and away from the neighborhood.

1.2 As you near the woods, a two-lane road intersects the trail under power lines. If you want to make this a loop, leave the Ptarmigan Peak Trail to the right (east) and follow the road. You can also stay the course on the main trail and use this as a descent trail. This route follows this access trail off the main trail. After passing a small aspen grove, this initially shoddy-looking trail morphs into a good hiking path.

4.2 Steady as she goes. This easy-to-follow trail cruises up and through the pines at a steady grade. At 4.2 miles, it closes the loop with the Ptarmigan Peak Trail and merges to a single path to the summit.

4.6 At 11,850 feet, there's a lonely sign designating the Ptarmigan Pass Trail. When summer grass is in bloom, this trail all but disappears, but it eventually fades in again closer to the pass (which is relatively easy to navigate to without a trail). If this intrigues you, read up on the variation at the end of this route description.

6.0 Ptarmigan's well-earned summit is broad and nearly flat. Return the way you came, and decide which way to descend at the spot where the two access trails merge.

7.8 Back at the fork in the path. To see new terrain (and take advantage of a few small but welcome creeks), go right along the Ptarmigan Peak Trail.

Of course, returning via the access trail is an option as well. As of November 2015, there was no sign at this juncture, but the trail split is obvious.
10.5 The trails reconnect. Depending on how you wandered to the summit, mileage may be slightly off here but only by 0.2–0.3 mile.
12.0 Return to the parking lot. You will likely figure out you can eschew the small access trail and just take the main road (Ptarmigan Trail) back to the parking area.

Variation

At mile 4.6, you can diverge toward Ptarmigan Pass, dropping down below the shoulder of Ptarmigan Peak. The trail comes and goes. Navigation here can be a little tricky, but the low point of the pass is evident as you continue northeast. The meadows below the pass are a great place to camp for a night. There are flat sections protected by pine groves and tiny alpine lakes fed by tiny alpine creeks. The trail to the pass magically reappears, only to disappear again as you head up the broad east slopes over UN 12,212 and up to Ptarmigan. This detour is 3.4 miles to the summit of Ptarmigan Peak, making your overall mileage (should you follow the standard trails down) closer to 13.5–13.8 miles. It's a nice circuit for strong hikers or mountain runners.

22. Ptarmigan Peak (12,498') via Laskey Gulch

Round-Trip Distance	8.6 miles
Class	2
Difficulty	6/10
Hiking Time	5–7 hours
Total Elevation Gain	3,360'
Terrain	Established trail gets faint in places but is easy to follow because it follows Laskey Gulch Creek.
Best Time to Climb	May–October

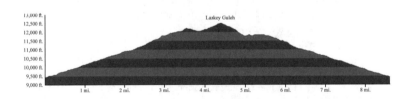

Overview Use extra caution when reaching this parking area (see "Driving Directions" for details). There are spots for about four or five vehicles. The trail up Laskey Gulch is surprisingly in good shape, despite the acres of beetle-killed pines along the way. Because it follows a creek all the way to the pass, it's an easy trail to follow even when it fades out here and there or if it has snow cover. This is a quiet, peaceful place. The shady forest is home to a lot of wildlife—photographers take note.

Mile/Route   **0.0** From the parking area, a worn trail switchbacks down and crosses the creek. From there, the trail simply and peacefully heads up Laskey Gulch. About 0.6 mile in, there is a large PTARMIGAN PEAK WILDERNESS sign designating the boundary for the wilderness area. Beyond that, this is a straightforward trail with no twists or turns.

2.7 The broad, open area below Ptarmigan Pass comes into view. This is a very private, secluded place to pitch a tent.

3.0 Ptarmigan Pass. Head off-trail and west to UN 12,212 before ascending the "big hill" that is Ptarmigan Peak.

3.4 The top of UN 12,212. Carry on west-northwest to Ptarmigan Peak's summit.

4.3 Ptarmigan's broad summit. Return the way you came, down to Ptarmigan Pass and back into Laskey Gulch. If you like off-trail navigation, the creeks that flow from the east side of Ptarmigan Peak all end up in Laskey Gulch, so consider this a shortcut if you're a decent navigator.

8.6 Finish.

Notes   Ptarmigan Peak Trailhead to Ptarmigan Peak then descending Laskey Gulch is a nice point-to-point, and it saves about 2 miles of hiking versus the out-and-back of the Ptarmigan Peak Trail. There's also the added benefit of being next to flowing water all the way down in Laskey Gulch (a plus on hot summer days, especially with dogs). Just be very, very careful with dogs at the Laskey Gulch parking area; it's too close for doggie comfort to I-70.

Ptarmigan Peak from the Ptarmigan Pass approach from Laskey Gulch

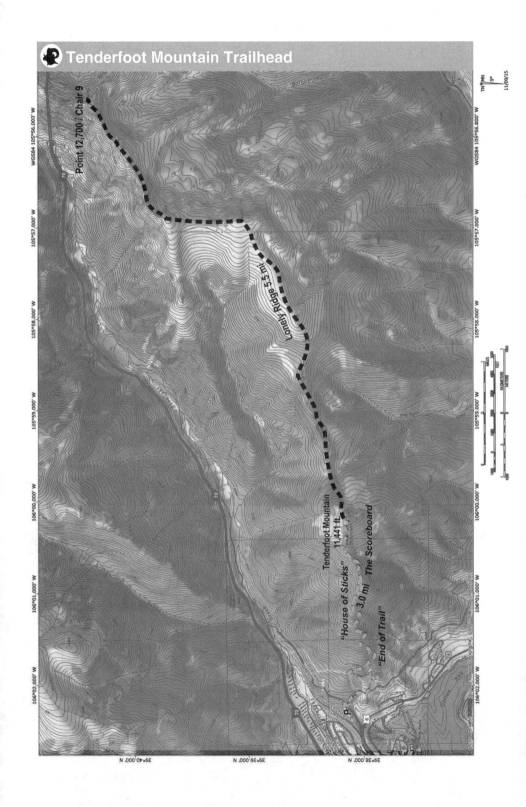

Tenderfoot Mountain Trailhead

Point 12,700 / Chair 9

Lonely Ridge 5.5 mi

Tenderfoot Mountain
11,441 ft

"House of Sticks"

3.0 mi The Scoreboard

"End of Trail"

WGS84 105°56.000' W
105°57.000' W
105°58.000' W
105°59.000' W
106°00.000' W
106°01.000' W
106°02.000' W

WGS84 105°56.800' W
105°57.000' W
105°58.000' W
105°59.000' W
106°00.000' W
106°01.000' W
106°02.000' W

N 39°40.000' N
N 39°39.000' N
N 39°38.000' N

TN MN
9°
11/09/15

Tenderfoot Mountain Trailhead (9,270')

This small mountain packs in a lot of adventure. Despite never breaking treeline, this is a scenic outing that involves a small section of confident off-trail navigation to reach the top. It's also a great quickie hike if you don't ascend to the summit (and there are acres of wild raspberries to be discovered in August). Tenderfoot also grants access to a ridgeline on the south side of I-70—probably the least-hiked mountains in this corridor.

PEAKS

- Tenderfoot Mountain: 11,441'
- "Lonely Ridge" Points: high point 12,700'

Wilderness Area and Range

White River National Forest, Front Range

Trailhead Distance from I-70

2.3 miles

Driving Directions

Westbound, take Exit 205 and go left at the exit onto US 6 E. If you are coming eastbound, take Exit 205 and turn right off the exit to get on US 6 E. Head up the hill 1.3 miles, passing the business district. At the light near the top of the hill, turn left onto Evergreen Road (for reference, Lake Dillon Drive is to the right of this lighted intersection). As soon as you leave US 6 toward Evergreen, take a fast right onto County Road 51. Follow this road 0.6 mile, past a water treatment facility on the right, where it turns to dirt. Just past the gated water tank is the Tenderfoot Mountain Trailhead on the right. If it's full, it's fine to park along the side of the road.

Vehicle Recommendations

Any vehicle can make this trailhead.

Fees/Camping

There are no fees to hike here. There are several nearby campgrounds at Lake Dillon Reservoir. Please visit townofdillon.com/index.aspx?page=71 for more information.

Dog Regulations

Dogs are requested to be on leash on the established, lower portion of this trail. Above that, they are allowed under voice control or on leash.

Summary

The Tenderfoot Mountain Trail is a funny one. The lower portion is a popular neighborhood hike, starting as an excellent Class 1 path that heads up to a bench and a beautiful viewpoint of Lake Dillon. Past that, it degrades into a loose, fractured trail in dark woods and then disappears altogether. Set a bearing to the "scoreboard" on the mountain. After a brief, uncertain off-trail section through the woods, hikers will tap into a rich series of ATV roads that makes for fine trails to the summit. Exploring beyond Tenderfoot heads up to a rarely visited spur ridge that tops out at Loveland Ski Area's Chair 9.

Primary Routes

23. ✪ Tenderfoot Mountain (11,441')

Round-Trip Distance	6 miles
Class	2
Difficulty	5/10
Hiking Time	3.5–5.0 hours
Total Elevation Gain	2,165'
Terrain	Nice trails lead to scrappy, Class 2 hills that are steep and loose. Eventually, some off-trail navigation is required before regaining a trail network to the summit.
Best Time to Climb	Year-round, though navigation is even trickier with snow on the ground.

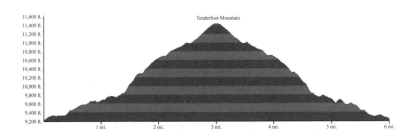

Overview Pine trees cover the entirety of this low-elevation dome, but don't let that deter you from visiting. There is some truth that it has inverse view potential: Many of the best views are from the lower portion of the hike before heading into the trees. Likewise, the off-trail segment of this hike is a good beginner's lesson in bearing navigation. A large, blank, green billboard (known informally as the scoreboard) sets a good beacon. Beyond it, trails reappear and lead to the top.

Mile/Route **0.0** Begin along the smooth dirt path of the lower Tenderfoot Trail. Do not take the thinner, less traveled trail to the left.

0.2 Shortly into the trail, split left to the Tenderfoot Trail. Talk about an instant reward! Vistas west to Lake Dillon and the peaks of the Tenmile Range, notably Peak 1 and Tenmile Peak, are incredible (especially in the morning sun). Continue on the trail as it switchbacks up through dark and lovely patches of aspen and lodgepole pine.

1.2 A little bench offers great viewpoints. The trail continues up the hill. So far, so good.

1.3 Not long after the bench, an ominous END OF TRAIL sign appears at 9,900 feet. This is not actually the end of the road, but it is the end of the easy stuff (and of the maintained trail). A loose, rocky trail continues up a steep hill. The Class 1 trail is done, and the Class 2 begins. At the top of the very

Dillon Reservoir as seen from the lower section of the Tenderfoot Mountain Trail. Peak One dominates the view to the west.

first steep hill, the trail splits. Go right to continue toward the summit. Go left to a short (0.1-mile) detour to some clear-cut power lines and the famous hidden fields of raspberries. Either way, continue right and up the trail. It's faint and continues up abrupt hills. A scoreboard looms on the hill above.

1.8 The trail reaches a flattish area where a few shabby piles of sticks are arranged at the base of pine trees. This "house of sticks" section is the end of the informal trail—it's time to bushwhack! Luckily, this is a short enterprise. The scoreboard is a good bearing to set, though if you've lost track of it, no worries. Stay to the right of the deeper forest but not too far downhill and continue up. Very faint trails may appear underfoot. After less than 0.2 mile, an extremely well-worn trail will appear. Huzzah!

2.0 Back on trails, head northeast back to the broad west ridge of Tenderfoot Mountain. Despite being ATV trails, these are actually quite nice paths through the woods. The area is slated to be revamped in 2016 (if you'd like more information, call the Dillon Ranger District at 970-468-5400 and ask about the Frey Gulch Trail restoration process).

Because the names of these trails will change, it's worth noting the trail to the top is designated as 9,509. Trail 9,514 is a short hook to the scoreboard base. Stay on Trail 9,509 to reach the summit. The scoreboard is at 10,800 feet, 2.1 miles in.

2.1 Bypass the scoreboard and continue up on Trail 9,509.

3.0 Top out on Tenderfoot Mountain's summit plateau at 11,441 feet. There are actual four-wheel-drive roads here that arrive via Frey Gulch to the east, but rarely is there much traffic, even on weekends (it's a tough jeep climb). A summit marker designating the highest point is in an open rock outcrop to the right (south).

Return the way you came. A GPS is helpful when entering the woods. Depending on where you hit Trail 9,509, you'll have a quick off-trail walk from the scoreboard back to the house of sticks. The rule here is to continue to bear west. Even if you miss the trail, you'll have good visual clues and will likely hit the power lines (if you completely botch it, which is tough to do). Note that Trail 9,509 was closed in winter 2016; otherwise, it would provide a straight shot south off the mountain.

4.3 Around this mileage, return to the house of sticks. Navigation back from here is easier, as it gains the access trail and then the actual Tenderfoot Trail. Remember at the last steep downhill, there is a split—left to the trail, right to delicious raspberries when they are in season.

6.0 Finish.

Notes   Fit hikers who are confident in route-finding can make this summit quickly. Trail runners, I'm looking at you! The ridge to the north looks inviting—if you want to challenge it all the way to the Continental Divide, it's 5.5 miles and an additional 2,400 feet of elevation gain with a bit of woods before gaining the accommodating terrain of "Lonely Ridge." A nice compromise is reaching the first point on the ridge, Point 12,196, which is well above treeline and 2.1 miles from the summit of Tenderfoot Mountain.

However, if you want to go for the divide, you'll reach it 8.5 miles from the start and 4,500 feet of total elevation gain. The top of the divide is 12,700 feet at Loveland Ski Area's Chair 9. The quickest descent is actually the point-to-point down Loveland Ski Area 3 miles to the parking area (see page 80). Otherwise, it's a 17-mile out-and-back round-trip. Yes, there's a reason it's called Lonely Ridge!

This is a good hike to use the free GPX tracks available at mountainouswords.com/I70-hikes.

XIV. Meadow Creek Trailhead (9,150')
and Ryan Gulch Trailhead (9,770')

*Buffalo Mountain's grand dome is the visual centerpiece of this pocket of east-
ern Gore Range Peaks. There are five high-quality summits from this duo of
trailheads, though Ryan Gulch is usually used exclusively to access Buffalo
Mountain. The Meadow Creek Trail goes up and over Eccles Pass, where excellent camping spots are bypassed on the way to the highest summit in this area,
13,189-foot Red Peak. Deming Mountain is an excellent, overlooked high point
that grants access to the sixth summit in this area, the tricky West Deming Peak.*

PEAKS

- Buffalo Mountain: 12,777'
- Sacred Buffalo: 12,755'
- Eccles Peak: 12,313'
- Red Peak: 13,189'
- Deming Mountain: 12,902'
- West Deming Peak: 12,736'

Wilderness Area and Range

Arapaho National Forest, Eagles Nest Wilderness, Front Range

Trailhead Distance from I-70

Ryan Gulch Trailhead: 3.5 miles
Meadow Creek Trailhead: 0.5 mile

Driving Directions

Ryan Gulch: Take Exit 205 from I-70 and head north on CO 9 about 100
feet (westbound) or a few hundred feet (eastbound) and turn west onto
Wildernest Road. Continue straight on this road as it turns into Buffalo
Mountain Drive. At 0.8 mile from the exit, turn left onto Buffalo Drive for
0.2 mile, then right back onto Wildernest Road. Continue on this road 1.8
miles as it winds through neighborhoods to the trailhead. Park on the left
side of the road and cross the street to begin the trail.

Meadow Creek: Exit I-70 at Exit 203 in Frisco. Approaching westbound, take a right off the exit into the roundabout and take the second
right (the first passes a private road) and follow it 0.5 mile on a dirt road
to the parking area. Eastbound, take a left at the exit ramp light and go
straight on Summit Boulevard to the roundabout and circle right, passing
the westbound exit ramp and the private road before turning right onto the
dirt access road. Go 0.5 mile to the trailhead.

Vehicle Recommendations

Any vehicle can make either of these trailheads.

Fees/Camping

There are no fees to hike or camp in this area.

Dog Regulations

Dogs must be on leash in the Eagle's Nest Wilderness and under voice control or on leash in Arapaho National Forest.

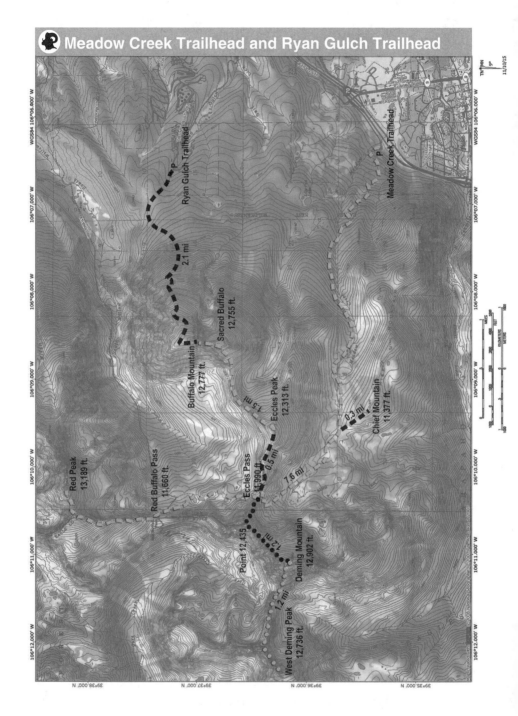

Meadow Creek Trailhead and Ryan Gulch Trailhead

Summary   If you're looking for a straightforward, enjoyable day hike in the mountains, Buffalo Mountain via Ryan Gulch is perfect. While it sees a good deal of traffic, the trail design is excellent, and crowds tend to disperse on the way up. The Meadow Creek Trailhead offers more variety. Deming Mountain and Eccles Peak (also called Eccles Mountain) are nice Class 2 walk-ups. Class 2+ Red Peak is a solid 15-mile round-trip but one that can be reasonably done as a day hike thanks to the quality of the trails leading to its summit. It's also possible to link these two trailheads for a great point-to-point excursion that goes over Sacred Buffalo (the south shoulder of Buffalo Mountain) and tackles a brief, thrillingly exposed Class 3 ridge between it and Buffalo Mountain. West Deming is the outlier in this group. It is a tough Class 3 traverse from Deming Mountain that has no easy way back—either regain Deming or drop down into one of the off-trail basins (for a LONG day).

Primary Routes

24. ❂ Buffalo Mountain (12,777') via Ryan Gulch

Round-Trip Distance	4.2 miles
Class	2
Difficulty	3/10
Hiking Time	3.5–5.0 hours
Total Elevation Gain	2,965'
Terrain	Very good out-and-back trail. The option to scramble over to Sacred Buffalo ups the ante with an exposed, Class 3 ridge on solid rock.
Best Time to Climb	June–October

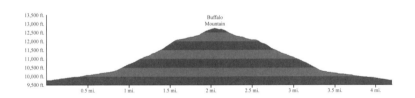

Overview   The Gore Range guards its summits with an array of difficult terrain, suspect rock, and long, difficult approaches. In contrast, Buffalo Mountain is a pleasant exception. It has one of the best mountain trails along the I-70 corridor. The views down to Lake Dillon are a novelty for Colorado mountain landscapes. This is a classic hike that gains a lot of elevation in a short distance. If you want to spice up your experience, the traverse over to Sacred Buffalo may take your breath away, thanks to the airy exposure along its brief ridge.

Mile/Route   0.0   Head out along the Buffalo Mountain Trail. In 0.2 mile, the trail enters the Eagles Nest Wilderness. Continue along the trail.

Eccles Pass, Eccles Peak, and the west ridge of Buffalo Mountain

0.5 At the signed four-way junction, stay left for the Buffalo Mountain Trail. From here, it's 1.6 miles to the top along the trail. There's 2,800 feet of elevation gain to be had; even though you are relatively close milewise, it's going to be work to get to the top. Toward the top, the excellent trail gets a little rockier but remains Class 2.

2.1 The summit. Great views abound. The ridge over to Sacred Buffalo to the south is surprisingly narrow. It's solid Class 3 on good rock with some wild exposure on both sides. Despite being a lower summit at 12,755 feet, the views from Sacred Buffalo are just as majestic. From this point, return the way you came—or consider making a point-to-point to Meadow Creek (see additional routes in this chapter). Once back atop Buffalo Mountain, return the way you came.

4.2 Finish.

Notes See the additional routes for information on climbing Buffalo via Sacred Buffalo's west ridge from Meadow Creek.

25. ✪ Red Peak (13,189') via Meadow Creek

Round-Trip Distance	15.1 miles
Class	2+
Difficulty	6/10
Hiking Time	7–10 hours
Total Elevation Gain	5,100'

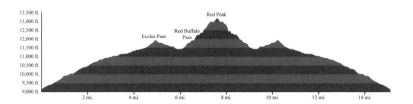

Terrain   Excellent trails for the majority of the route. The final 1.3 miles are along a Class 2+ ridge with a bit of light scrambling.

Best Time to Climb   **June–October**

Overview   If you have the legs, I have your mountain! Despite the long mileage, fit hikers will be able to do this adventure as a day hike in reasonable time. If you want to make this a two-day outing, the camping on either side of Eccles Pass is exceptional. Peaceful alpine ponds, open meadows, and sheltered pockets of trees with flat spots are perfect for spending a night out then grabbing the summit the following morning. The hike and scramble up Red Peak is on solid rock and gives a nice sampling of the more accommodating side of the western Gore Range peaks.

Mile/Route   **0.0**   The Meadow Creek Trail starts at the kiosk at the parking area. It's 4.4 miles to the lower reaches of Eccles Pass. Along the way, pass through aspen groves, pine forests, and finally a series of ponds before the basin opens up.

4.4   The Gore Range Trail splits off to the left—more on where it goes in the "Extra Credit" section on page 120. For Red Peak, stay the course and follow the trail up to the saddle of Eccles Pass.

5.0   At 11,900 feet, you will reach the summit of Eccles Pass. Red Peak towers to the north. Did you enjoy the warm-up? The day is just getting started! One glance down into the basin to the north will show why it's such a good camping area. Continue on the excellent trail down to pristine alpine ponds.

5.8   At the largest of the three lakes, you can save a little bit of distance and time by taking the access trail left at the north end of the lake. It heads up to Red Buffalo Pass (as does the established trail), but it cuts off a bit of downhill hiking that has to regain a bit of elevation. You have a big enough day already! If you want to stay on the main trail, that's fine too; both go to the pass.

6.3   Red Buffalo Pass is the saddle between Red Peak and the north ridge of Deming Mountain that sits at 11,660 feet. Leave the trail and set off north on the ridge. There are bits and pieces of hiker's trails, and they tend to follow the logical lines. The scrambling is easy on mostly good rock, and exposure is low.

7.3   Point 13,005 is a false summit, but thankfully it's easy going from here to the top of Red Peak. It's difficult to see if the true summit of Red Peak is on the near or far side of a nasty-looking notch in the distance. Luckily, it's the closer of the two. From Point 13,005, bear northeast down to a saddle then up to the top. Some light scrambling is required.

7.6 At long last, the summit! While all the views are spectacular, looking west is especially impressive. The deeply forested Gore Creek Trail carves its way to Vail. Beyond that, the jagged profiles of the western Gore peaks dare you to explore their isolated kingdom.

Return the way you came, staying on the ridges down to Red Buffalo Pass. Pay attention to the weather—there is still the matter of clearing Eccles Pass a second time, and it's no place to be caught in a lightning storm. There are plenty of safe outposts in the basin west of Eccles Pass if you need them. Otherwise, carry on.

10.3 Back at the summit of Eccles Pass. Continue on Meadow Creek Trail.

10.8 The Gore Range split. Stay left and head down to the parking lot.

15.1 Finish.

Notes The camping on either side of Eccles Pass makes this an inviting two-day outing, even if you have the legs and lungs to do it as a day hike. A three-day summer weekend getting Red Peak, Deming Mountain, and Eccles Peak is mountain bliss—though to that end, so is pitching a tent and peacefully reading a book in the shadow of these great mountains.

Red Peak from
Eccles Pass

26. ✪ Deming Mountain (12,902') and Eccles Peak (12,313') via Meadow Creek

Round-Trip Distance	13.2 miles (options to do less by skipping one of the peaks)
Class	2
Difficulty	6/10
Hiking Time	6–8 hours
Total Elevation Gain	4,440'
Terrain	High-quality trail to technically easy, off-trail Class 2 scrambles.
Best Time to Climb	June–October

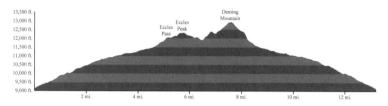

Overview Much like Red Peak, this adventure starts with a prelude hike to Eccles Pass. Eccles Peak is the easier of the two peaks to grab, so it's the best one to do first. Deming Mountain has some light scrambling and steep, grassy slopes. If you've hiked Peak 1 (or plan to), this is an interesting perspective of the base of the Tenmile Range. Deming Mountain was named after Frisco resident John Deming, who lived in the area 1890–1924. His present-day family is still in Colorado and hikes the peak once a year as a family tradition.

Mile/Route 0.0 Start at the Meadow Creek Trail and follow it 5.0 miles to the top of Eccles Pass. It's a fast 5 miles, if there is such a thing, because the trail is well maintained and straightforward.

4.4 Pass the Gore Range Trail split on your left and continue to Eccles Pass.

5.0 The top of Eccles Pass at 11,990 feet. At this point, decide if you want to snag both peaks or the single summit of your choice. Eccles is the easier option, so it's a good place to start. Go off-trail and head east 0.5 mile to the rounded summit of Eccles Peak.

5.5 Eccles Peak as a cairn and summit register. It's 12,313 feet but is totally dwarfed by Sacred Buffalo to the east, which looks enormous from this perspective. Views west here provide a nice overview of the traverse over to Deming. Return to Eccles Pass.

6.0 Back at Eccles Pass. Time to head west! First up is the scramble to Point 12,435, 0.6 mile away.

6.6 Point 12,435 lines up for a nice walk over to Deming's summit. Aim southwest along the broad ridge and carry on.

7.2 Deming's summit. See the "Notes" section on the next page if you want to give West Deming Peak a whirl, but be warned it adds a mountain of work, pun intended. Otherwise, return back the way you came. It's

Looking west to Deming Mountain

possible to traverse the slopes off of Point 12,435 rather than go all the way back to Eccles Pass. They are steep but solid, and the way back to the Meadow Creek Trail will be visually obvious. Once you reach it, follow it back to the parking area.

13.2 Finish.

Notes West Deming was a prickly addition to this guide. The ridge connecting it off the west side of Deming Mountain has sections that could be Class 3 or 4 depending on your route-finding, but that's not the main issue. It's 1.2 miles from Deming, but the ridge drops 854 feet before regaining 730 feet back to the top—and then you have to get back. The obvious way is to reclimb Deming, which grinds back up the 854 feet you dropped. It's 2.4 total extra miles from Deming and more than 1,700 vertical feet.

One descent option: dropping off the steep slopes to the north toward Red Buffalo Pass, but that means a gnarly mile in loose, large boulders— not recommended! Heading to the low saddle between Deming and West Deming offers an out down the loose, sandy slopes into Tenmile Creek Basin (see "Extra Credit" on page 120 for more info on this trailhead).

Extra Credit: North Tenmile Creek Trailhead

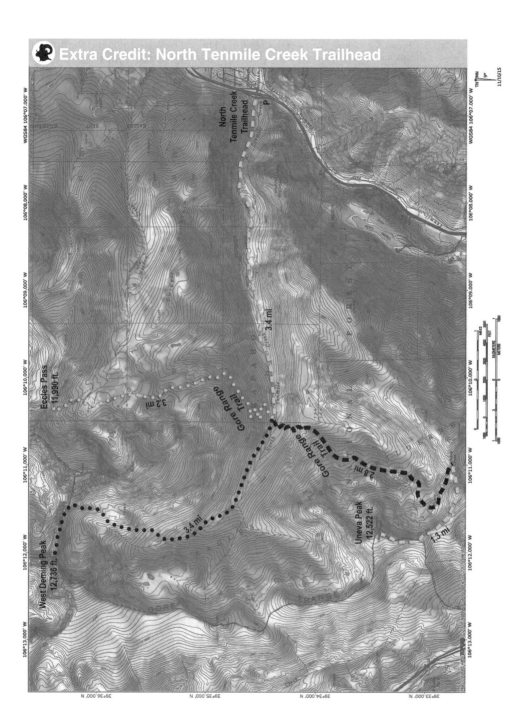

North Tenmile Creek Trailhead

P

Eccles Pass
11,990 ft.

Gore Range Trail

3.4 mi

3.2 mi

Gore Range Trail

2.8 mi

West Deming Peak
12,736 ft.

3.4 mi

Uneva Peak
12,522 ft.

1.3 mi

GORE RANGE

11/10/15

From the saddle, it's 1.4 miles of off-trail hiking before gaining the North Tenmile Creek Trail, then 5.9 more on-trail miles to the North Tenmile Creek Trailhead—more than 14.2 miles total.

But there is another way to get West Deming that is not as demanding—via Vail Pass and Uneva Peak. See page 153 for details on this option (probably the best way to get West Deming).

See page 153 for details on this option

Meadow Creek to Ryan Gulch Buffalo-Style Traverse

Class 2 with brief Class 3 section – 9.2 miles – 4,370' elevation gain

This point-to-point cruises up Eccles Pass from Meadow Creek, then heads over Eccles Peak and powers up the steep, rocky west slopes of Sacred Buffalo. The most challenging section is the Class 3 0.2-mile ridge between Sacred Buffalo and Buffalo Mountain—it's solid but exposed. From there, walk off Buffalo's standard route.

Chief Mountain (11,377')

A bonus peak, this named summit is 0.3 mile off of the Meadow Creek Trail. It's an off-trail detour you can make about 3 miles into the Meadow Creek Trail after passing the first set of ponds as the basin opens up into an alpine meadow. See the map on page 112 for details.

See the map on page 112 for details.

North Tenmile Creek Trailhead (see map on page 119)

(see map on page 119)

This is a very easy-to-reach trailhead. Westbound on I-70, take Exit 201. At the end of the exit ramp, trailhead parking is on the right. Eastbound, it's Exit 201, then left off the exit and under the highway to the trailhead.

While it's a nice and scenic hike, North Tenmile Creek Trail serves as a secondary way to access several peaks, including Deming Mountain and Uneva Peak via the Gore Range Trail (which it connects to 3.4 miles in). Going north on the Gore Range Trail eventually connects to the junction below Eccles Pass mentioned in the Red Peak description. Going South leads to Uneva Pass and eventually Uneva Peak. A point-to-point to Wheeler Lakes/Copper Mountain parking is possible. Extending to the end of the basin makes a 12-mile out-and-back to West Deming Peak possible via the Deming–West Deming saddle.

The point is that this is not the most efficient trailhead for peak bagging, but it is a wonderful access point for backpacking and alternative routes. If this were a backpacking guide, it would have glowing reviews. For day hikers, it can either be incorporated as a point-to-point trailhead or a longer, tougher way to grab a few summits (Uneva Pass to Uneva Peak is the most logical). The one plus for this "style" of grabbing peaks is that many of the harder Gore Range summits have similar distances and off-trail challenges—so think of the North Tenmile Creek Trail as a good training ground for the more difficult western Gores.

XV. Peak 1 Trailhead (9,120') and Miners Creek Trailhead (9,760')

Peak 1 and summits beyond make up the very best extended Class 3 ridge scramble along I-70. It's a solid workout to reach Peak 1 and the traverse over to Peak 4 requires good route-finding. Views down to Lake Dillon to the east and Copper Mountain to the west will linger in your memory long after you've left the high mountains. Connecting as a point-to-point to Miners Creek is an excellent, sturdy day hike. Other point-to-point options include traversing to the Far East Trailhead via the Colorado Trail or running the Tenmile Ridge to Breckenridge. Of course, out-and-backs to Peak 1 are fun, and if you don't have two vehicles, looping these peaks is still possible.

PEAKS

- Peak 1: 12,805'
- Tenmile Peak (Peak 2): 12,933'
- Peak 3: 12,676'
- Peak 4: 12,866'

- Peak 5: 12,855'
- Peak 6: 12,573'
- Royal Mountain: 10,502'

Wilderness Area and Range

Arapaho National Forest, Tenmile Range

Trailhead Distance from I-70

Peak 1 Trailhead: 0.1 mile

Miners Creek Trailhead: 2.3 miles

Driving Directions

Peak 1: Take Exit 201. If exiting westbound, go left off the exit, under the I-70 bridge, and past the eastbound exit. Take the next right into a paved parking area. Eastbound, simply take a right off the exit then a quick right to the parking lot. This lot is used to access the bike path and has a restroom. Overnight parking and in-your-vehicle camping is allowed, but you cannot pitch a tent here.

Miners Creek: Take Exit 203 toward Frisco. Westbound, go through the roundabout and take CO 9/Summit Boulevard toward Frisco. Eastbound, simply take a right at the light at the end of the exit to get to the same place. Follow this road through Frisco 1.7 miles. At the stoplight intersection, turn right onto Peak 1 Boulevard/County Road 2004 (look for the brick WATER DANCE sign to the left of this intersection as a clue because the print on the road sign is very small).

Go 0.1 mile and take a right onto a paved road (just before a crosswalk) then a quick left onto the paved Miners Creek Road. At 0.2 mile, the lower trailhead for Miner's Creek is on the left—but even passenger cars can go farther up this road. Reset your odometer.

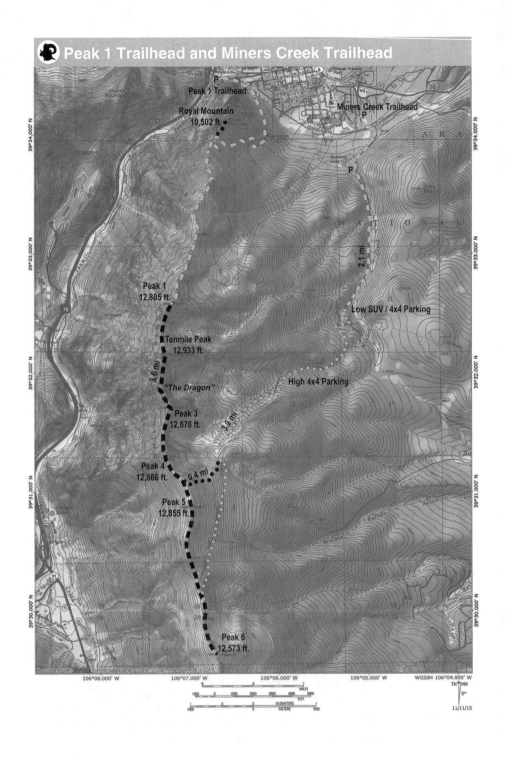

Peak 1 Trailhead and Miners Creek Trailhead

Peak 1 Trailhead

Miners Creek Trailhead

Royal Mountain
10,502 ft.

Peak 1
12,805 ft.

Tenmile Peak
12,933 ft.

Low SUV / 4x4 Parking

"The Dragon"

Peak 3
12,676 ft.

High 4x4 Parking

Peak 4
12,866 ft.

0.4 mi

Peak 5
12,855 ft.

Peak 6
12,573 ft.

2.1 mi

3.6 mi

3.9 mi

WGS84 106°04.000' W
11/11/15

It's going to feel like you are breaking the law, but as long as the access gate is open, continue on the paved road/bike path. Yes, it's 100% legal, and yes, it's going to feel strange. Be very careful for cyclists as the main Frisco Bike Path crosses a few hundred feet past the lower trailhead. Stay on the paved road until it bends right and turns to dirt. There's a parking area, but most passenger cars can continue 1.2 miles to the Rainbow Lake Trailhead, a good place to park. SUVs, SUCs, and four-wheel drives can continue along the road. It gets steeper but remains in good shape—high clearance helps with the water drainage humps. At mile 2.1 is an improvised parking area (good place to car camp) and the best place for SUVs or SUCs to park. Four-wheel drives and tough SUVs can continue another 1.2 miles to the high parking, but the hills get much steeper, much rockier, and more rutted. SUVs can get up this stuff, but it's going to put some real wear and tear on your truck. High parking is at the end of the road around 10,800 feet.

Vehicle Recommendations Any vehicle can make the Peak 1 Trailhead. Passenger cars can make the lower parking at Miners Creek. SUVs/SUCs can make the upper parking area, while tough SUVs and true four-wheel-drive vehicles can make the high parking.

Fees/Camping There are no fees to hike or camp in this area. Note that parking/camping is not allowed on the lower sections of Miners Creek Road except where designated.

Dog Regulations Dogs are allowed under voice control or on leash. Pups must be on leash on the Frisco Bike Path.

Summary There are many ways to explore these peaks. The adventure potential is huge, ranging from day hikes to epic traverses. Experienced mountain explorers can link together Peaks 1–10 or make point-to-points back to Frisco or Copper Mountain. The views and quality of scrambling are top notch between Peaks 1 and 4.

Primary Routes

27. ✪ Peak 1 (12,805') to Peak 6 (12,573') Point-to-Point

Round-Trip Distance	11.3 miles
Class	3
Difficulty	8/10
Hiking Time	7–9 hours
Total Elevation Gain	5,600'
Terrain	Good, steep trails to Peak 1 then Class 3 scrambling on semi-exposed, solid rock along the ridges.
Best Time to Climb	June–September

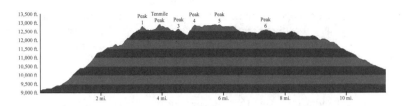

Overview While this route is written as a point-to-point, there are lots of options here. Simply doing Peak 1 as an out-and-back (7.2 miles) or Peak 1–Tenmile Peak out-and-back (8.7 miles) are good day hikes. But the best part of this adventure is the full traverse from Peak 1 to Peak 4—a thrilling, Class 3 scramble. After Peak 4, the terrain mellows out to broad slopes, so if you're in it for the scrambling, dropping off Peak 4 to Miners Creek makes perfect sense (it's 7.8 miles versus 11.3 miles for the full traverse to Peak 6). The walk over to Peak 6 from Peak 4 is a nice way to extend the day, and the hike back is along the Colorado Trail for a while. See "Notes" on page 127 for information on linking this route with the Far East Trailhead.

This route assumes one vehicle parked at the SUV/upper parking on Miners Creek Road and starting at the Peak 1 Trailhead. Parking lower on Miners Creek Road will add miles. If you only have one vehicle, it's possible to walk back to the Peak 1 Trailhead via the Frisco Bike Path. It's roughly 13.5 miles back to the bike path on Miners Creek Road, then another 2.5 miles on the bike path to the parking area. I have done this route by locking up my mountain bike at the Miners Creek SUV parking area in the morning and riding the bike back to the Peak 1 Trailhead after hiking—a fun duathlon option. Accordingly, you can leave your vehicle at Miners Creek and bike over to the Peak 1 Trailhead and retrieve your bike on the way back.

Mile/Route **0.0** From the Peak 1 parking area, go left onto the paved bike path, following it southeast 0.3 mile to the Mount Royal Trail that begins off the bike path.
0.3 Turn right onto the Mount Royal/Peak 1 Trail. Stay on the wide main trail, ignoring the network of side trails that split off.
1.0 Here are the sparse ruins of Masontown, an old mining camp that was destroyed by avalanches three times before people realized it wasn't the best location for a town. There isn't much to see here—a few brick foundations and some debris. Carry on the main, wide trail—it's going to get steep here.
1.5 Feel the burn! Here, the trail splits left and goes straight—you can take either. The left path explores a few old mining cabins and links back to the main trail in about 0.2 mile. Staying straight bypasses this. There is a hiker's trail (0.1 mile) over to Royal Mountain, a nice little lookout that is really just a bump on Peak 1's shoulder. Visit if you like . . . or not. Carry on the main trail as it begins to breach treeline.
2.6 The famous "radio shack" is along the trail. Cell phone reception is excellent here. Carry on the trail, which narrows a bit but persists along the flanks of Peak 1 to the summit.
3.4 The trail switches to the west side of the peak, where the grey rock and dark shadows create a different aura from the sunny, pine-lined path on the

east side. Some light scrambling may be required but the terrain stays Class 2 to the summit of Peak 1.

3.6 Peak 1's summit—how was *that* for a warm-up?! The real work is about to begin. From here, the rule of thumb is to either stay on the solid ridgeline rock or head to the west side to bypass technical rock sections. The first segment to Tenmile Peak is the easiest of the Class 3 terrain. Head south down to a low gully and scamper on good rock to Tenmile Peak (the highest summit of the day at 12,933 feet).

4.3 Tenmile Peak's lofty summit! It becomes clear that linking Peak 3 and Peak 4 is going to be some work. Never fear, the path will reveal itself as you proceed.

4.4 A short distance after descending south off Tenmile Peak, you will encounter "the Dragon." This is a neat spine of rock that begins after reaching the low saddle between Tenmile Peak and Peak 3. If you want to "ride the Dragon," it's Class 4/low Class 5 climbing with some tricky down-climbs. The Class 3 option is to stay right (west) of the dragon and bypass it—there's a faint trail that twists through the boulders. Regain the ridge at any point past the Dragon. Route-finding is required to keep it at Class 3, though there's easy Class 4 and always an option to back off if you feel too exposed or uncertain. Pass the Dragon and scramble up to Peak 3 on the solid ridgeline.

Dr. Jon Kedrowski approaches the head of the "Dragon."

A look at the elegant ridge-lines along the Tenmile Range

4.6 The summit of Peak 3! The scramble over to Peak 4 eases up a bit. Staying on the direct ridgeline is the best way to get there. The rock is good, the views are stunning—this is mountain scrambling at its best.

5.2 Peak 4 at least! Don't forget to grab a photo of the traverse from Peak 1. This is a great time to descend (off-trail) along Peak 4's east slopes to connect with the Miners Creek/Colorado Trail. It's 2.6 miles to the upper parking lot from here. Make certain to stay on the Miners Creek Trail/Miners Creek Road when it splits from the Colorado Trail. The two do share a common trail for some time, up to the high four-wheel-drive parking.

If you're still ready for more peaks, enjoy the walk over to Peak 5— easy Class 1 along broad slopes.

5.8 Peak 5 is the fifth peak of the day. Between Peaks 5 and 6, the shared Miners Creek Trail/Colorado Trail appears and will lead you the last few feet to the summit of Peak 6, 1.4 miles away.

7.2 The six-pack is complete—the summit of Peak 6! To walk out, follow the Miners Creek/Colorado Trail right (east) off the summit. When the Colorado Trail splits near the high four-wheel-drive parking, stay on the Miners Creek Trail/Miners Creek Road. After all the hard work, this is a nice ending to a long day.

11.3 Finish at the SUV/upper parking area on Miners Creek Road.

Notes   A fun option that avoids all the four-wheel-drive road nonsense is to leave a car at the Far East Trailhead (see page 129) as your second vehicle. This can be done with any passenger vehicle. Once you hit the Colorado Trail, rather than descend to the east, stay on the Colorado Trail to the west and follow it to the Far East Parking across from Copper Mountain. This option is 10.4 miles total and may be the better of the point-to-points, but it will require a bit more driving distancewise (which may equate to about the same timewise).

If you want to go big time, the Peak 1–10 traverse can be done a couple of different ways. Leave one vehicle at Breckenridge Ski Area (preferred) or Mayflower Gulch. Just getting to Peak 10 is 10.7 miles and 8,000 feet of elevation gain! From there, descend the Breck Ski. Or if you're really, really ready for the big time, traverse down Peak 10 to the saddle between it and Crystal Peak. At this point, you're already in beast mode, so what's another 700 vertical feet to climb 13,852-foot Crystal Peak? Return to vehicle two at Mayflower Gulch for over 14.7 miles of fun. Yet more options: you could descend west off Crystal Peak into the Crystal Lake Basin and gain the Wheeler Trail, bypass Francie's Hut, and reach the Spruce Creek parking area, about 13.9 miles total.

And if you're going for an elite traverse—often undertaken over two days—the entire Tenmile traverse is a hoot. From Peak 10, it adds on Crystal Peak, Pacific Peak, Atlantic Peak, optionally Fletcher Mountain, and concludes along the thrilling Class 3 west ridge of Quandary Peak at the standard route parking for Quandary Peak off Hoosier Pass. It's 19 total miles and 11,660 feet of elevation gain. A good overnight place to pitch a tent is west of the Crystal–Pacific saddle, though you'll be sleeping well over 12,000 feet—so acclimate before going for this adventure. The ridge between Atlantic and Fletcher is a mess, Class 4 and Class 5 on bad rock, so the safer Class 3 option is to drop off the east slopes of Atlantic and swing around to the Fletcher/Quandary saddle and summit Fletcher via its Class 2 southeast ridge—then get Quandary. Since this is Colorado, I have no doubt people do this entire thing in a single day—I've only done it as a two-day adventure.

Additional Route

Miners Creek Peak 4, Peak 5, and Peak 6 Direct

Class 2 – 6.8 miles – 3,100' elevation gain

What does a guy/gal/dog have to do to get a summit that isn't a lung-burning, quad-melting hike? Try the direct lines up to Peaks 4, 5, and 6. From the upper Miners Creek parking, take the Miners Creek Trail up 2.4 miles to about 11,800 feet. This will be above treeline. Then, hit up the slopes directly to the saddle between Peaks 4 and 5. Or go ahead and stay on the Miners Creek/Colorado Trail to Peak 6 and loop back to Peaks 5 and 4. From the high four-wheel-drive parking, this is a great half-day option as it cuts out 2 miles of foot travel. If you're up for a tour, adding on Peak 7 and Peak 8 makes this a bigger day but keeps it all at Class 1–2.

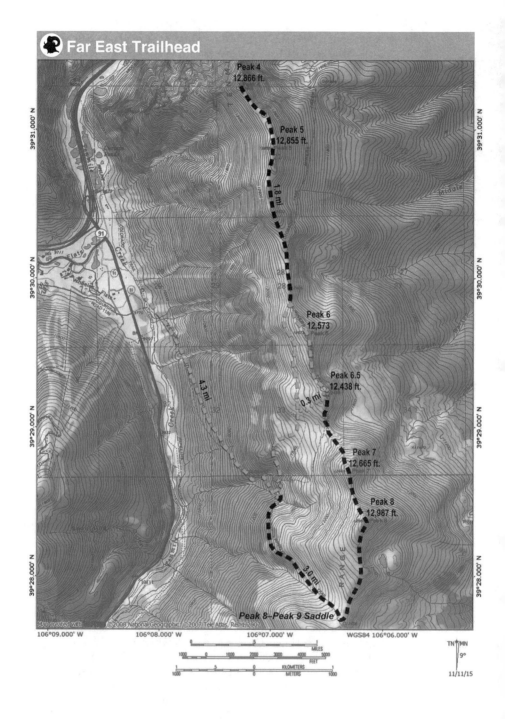

Far East Trailhead

Peak 4
12,866 ft.

Peak 5
12,855 ft.

1.8 mi

Peak 6
12,573

Peak 6.5
12,438 ft.

0.3 mi

4.3 mi

Peak 7
12,665 ft.

Peak 8
12,987 ft.

3.0 mi

Peak 8–Peak 9 Saddle

106°09.000' W   106°08.000' W   106°07.000' W   WGS84 106°06.000' W

39°31,000' N
39°30,000' N
39°29,000' N
39°28,000' N

MILES
FEET
KILOMETERS
METERS

TN MN
9°
11/11/15

Far East Trailhead (9,770')

The Colorado Trail will be your guide from this nifty trailhead. Head up to a ridgeline in the heart of the Tenmile Range, where you will wander along high, broad alpine hills. Peak 4 to Peak 6.5 have mellow terrain, while Peaks 7 and 8 are a bit steeper but still easy to follow. Far East is an excellent destination for an out-and-back day hike or as one destination for a point-to-point adventure.

PEAKS

- Peak 6: 12,573'
- Peak 6.5: 12,438'
- Peak 7: 12,665'
- Peak 8: 12,987'
- Peak 5: 12,855'
- Peak 4: 12,866'

Wilderness Area and Range

Arapaho National Forest, Tenmile Range

Trailhead Distance from I-70

1.2 miles

Driving Directions

Take Exit 195 from I-70 to CO 91 S. Westbound traffic will just continue straight, while eastbound will take a right at the end of the exit. Follow this road 1.1 miles and pull off left (east) to the Copper Mountain overflow parking (access to the trailhead is allowed even when the Copper lot is closed). Drive to the far east side of the lot and continue south (right) where the marked Far East Trailhead is.

Vehicle Recommendations

Any vehicle can make this trailhead.

Fees/Camping

There are no fees to camp or hike here. Technically, there is no camping allowed in the Copper overflow lot, but tent camping is allowed about 70 feet east of the lot on the far side of the bike path in the woods.

Dog Regulations

Dogs are allowed under voice control or on leash.

Summary

The Colorado Trail grants access above treeline and the broad, rolling ridgeline. Beyond that, you are free to roam. Terrain along the way is Class 1, a rare phenomenon when off-trail routes are required. Ambitious hikers can actually grab Peaks 4, 5, 6, 6.5, 7, and 8 and return via Wheeler Trail for a longer day. If you are looking for a low-commitment, high-reward hike, this is it—these peaks offer an elevated sanctuary from the busy traffic below. A simple out-and-back to Peak 6.5 is the quickest summit to grab, but chances are you'll be inclined to wander once you are up here.

28. ⊘ Peak 6 (12,573') and Peak 6.5 (12,438') Tour

Round-Trip Distance	7.5 miles
Class	1
Difficulty	3/10
Hiking Time	4.5–6.0 hours
Total Elevation Gain	3,000'
Terrain	Well-cared-for trail up to broad, open mountain slopes.
Best Time to Climb	June–October

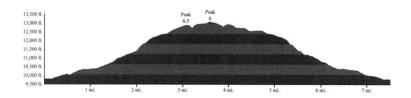

Overview While the 3,000 feet of elevation is work, it's done along the Class 1 Colorado Trail. What little off-trail navigation there is never leaves the line of sight of the established trails. This basic tour is the foundation for optional adventures to Peaks 4, 5, 7, and 8. This is an excellent option for a peaceful day with friends and dogs. It's also a popular destination for trail runners and mountain bikers, though the trails are rarely busy. From the ridgeline, views extend east to Lake Dillon Reservoir to Grays and Torreys Peaks, while the western perspective looks out on Copper Mountain Ski Area and the distant Sawatch and Gore Range summits. The cracked top of Pacific Peak dominates the southern landscape, while Deming Mountain and Red Peak round out the northern vista.

Mile/Route **0.0** Walk a short bit left (north) on the paved bike path to reach the well-signed start of the Colorado Trail. Cross the bridge and begin the adventure, heading south toward one big switchback. Enjoy the peacefulness of the forest. The trail is very easy to follow.

2.0 At a bend in the trail, the Wheeler Trail comes in from the south. If you want to visit Peak 8 (or Peak 9 for that matter), the Wheeler Trail goes to a saddle between the two. See "Notes" on the next page for more details. Stay on the Colorado Trail as it turns north and heads up to treeline.

2.5 Treeline starts to give way to glorious alpine hillside, especially when deep orange sunlight is illuminating the landscape in the early morning. There is a split to the Miners Creek Trail, which essentially goes the same place as this route: Peak 6.5. Again, where to wander is up to you—leave the trail and head up to Peak 6.5 (UN 12,438), walk up to Peak 7 to the south, the choice is yours. For this route, stay on the Colorado Trail as it traverses north below Peak 6.5 to Peak 6.

Hiking toward Peak 6 with Crystal and Pacific Peaks in the background

3.8 Peak 6's summit. Options to hike north to Peaks 5 and 4, which would be 3.6 additional miles out-and-back but only add on 500 vertical feet for two additional summits. It's 0.5 mile down to Peak 6.5.

4.3 Peak 6.5's summit. Don't monkey with the ski patrol storage gear. Walk the slopes west back down to the Colorado Trail (easily visible) and close the lollipop loop.

7.5 Finish.

Notes At Peak 6.5, those who want to carry on south can walk up the steep-but-fair north slopes of Peak 7 (0.4 mile from Peak 6.5) over to Peak 8 (0.9 mile away). Walking off the south slopes of Peak 8 brings hikers to the Wheeler Trail at the saddle between Peaks 8 and 9 (1.8 miles). Hang a right and proceed 1.2 miles back to the intersection with the Colorado Trail.

As mentioned in the Peak 1 Trailhead and Miners Creek Trailhead chapter (see "Notes" on page 127), Far East is a great place to use as one terminus of a point-to-point adventure. Peak 1 from Peak 1 Trailhead to Peak 6 and down to Far East is a perfect option. Another interesting route is to take the Wheeler Trail on the ascent and grab Peak 9, Peak 10, and Crystal Peak, descending to Mayflower Gulch as the other finishing point.

Come winter, Peak 6 is an access point for side-country terrain from Breckenridge Mountain, including the famous "SKY" chutes (next time you come down the east of Vail Pass, note how the chutes through the trees on the hillside seem to make out the letters S-K-Y).

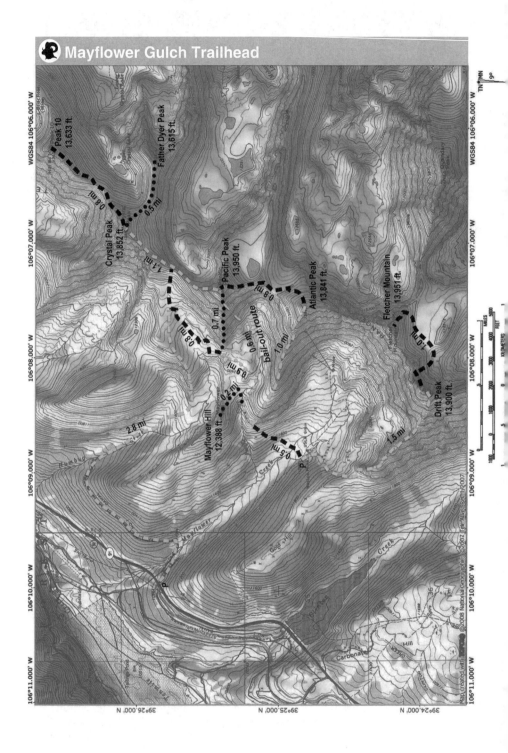

Peak 10
13,633 ft.

Father Dyer Peak
13,615 ft.

0.8 mi

0.5 mi

Crystal Peak
13,852 ft.

1.1 mi

Pacific Peak
13,950 ft.

0.7 mi

0.8 mi

Atlantic Peak
13,841 ft.

0.8 mi

0.6 mi
bail-out route

1.0 mi

Fletcher Mountain
13,951 ft.

1.0 mi

0.9 mi

0.2 mi

Mayflower Hill
12,388 ft.

Drift Peak
13,900 ft.

2.8 mi

0.5 mi

1.5 mi

TN MN
9°

Map created with TOPO! ©2008 National Geographic (www.topo.com) ©2007

XVII. Mayflower Gulch Trailhead (11,500')

Mayflower Gulch is the ultimate "build your own adventure" trailhead. Eight excellent summits are waiting to be claimed by a variety of routes. Interestingly, none of them have established trails (partially due to mining claims in the area). The scrambling on these peaks is top-notch, most notably on the airy, exposed west ridge of Pacific Peak. The trio of Crystal–Pacific–Atlantic may be the very best combined hiking/scrambling route in Colorado. Besides the summit appeal, the mining history in the basin area makes for a good add-on adventure.

PEAKS

- Pacific Peak: 13,950'
- Atlantic Peak: 13,841'
- Crystal Peak: 13,852'
- Drift Peak: 13,900'
- Fletcher Mountain: 13,951'
- Mayflower Hill: 12,388'
- Father Dyer Peak: 13,615'
- Peak 10: 13,633'

Wilderness Area and Range

Arapaho National Forest, Tenmile Range

Trailhead Distance from I-70

7.8 miles

Driving Directions

Take Exit 195 toward Copper Mountain to CO 91S (toward Fremont Pass). The turnoff for Mayflower Gulch is 5.9 miles. As you ascend the hill, the large, paved parking area is on the left. This is the passenger car parking. SUVs, four-wheel drives, and high-clearance SUCs can continue along the Mayflower Gulch Road 1.5 miles to the upper parking at the Boston Mine ruins. Tough SUVs and four-wheel drives can scrap up the Gold Hill access road here to gain access to some nice car camping spots and the top of Gold Hill (0.5 mile).

Vehicle Recommendations

Any vehicle can make the lower parking. SUVS, high-clearance SUCs, and four-wheel drives can make the upper parking no problem. The road is mostly flat and rutted out in a few spots, but as far as four-wheel-drive roads go, this one is in pretty good shape. The car parking lot (paved) is a good place to park for any vehicle if you are aiming to hike just Crystal Peak or the Crystal–Father Dyer–Peak 10 combo.

Fees/Camping

There are no fees to hike or camp here. The car camping (or near-the-car camping in some cases) is good at the upper parking area. The Humbug Creek Basin is a nice place to pitch a day if you want to backpack in a bit.

Dog Regulations

Dogs are allowed under voice control or on leash.

Summary Mayflower Gulch is the perfect place to mix and match ridgelines and summits. The tamest route in the area would be an out-and-back on Atlantic Peak's west ridge—3.2 miles round-trip. For the longer traverses, it's a good idea to be acclimated before giving them a go—most involve several hours of demanding hiking above 13,000 feet. Besides the high ridges, touring the basins below these peaks is a treat. Great meadows of wildflowers, quiet streams, and solid boulder fields add to the adventure.

There are many ways to combine these routes. See the Atlantic–Pacific–Crystal Traverse "Notes" on page 137 for more details. Some of the land in the basin is owned by the Climax Mine, which generously offers public access—let's hope that doesn't change.

Primary Routes

29. ✪ Atlantic (13,841')–Pacific (13,950')–Crystal (13,852') Traverse

Round-Trip Distance	6.1 miles
Class	2+ with a short Class 3 section off the summit of Pacific Peak
Difficulty	8/10
Hiking Time	7–9 hours
Total Elevation Gain	3,560'
Terrain	Off-trail basin walks that include boulder fields. Ridges are rocky, mostly solid, and relatively easy to follow. Short Class 3 section off the top of Pacific Peak.
Best Time to Climb	June–September

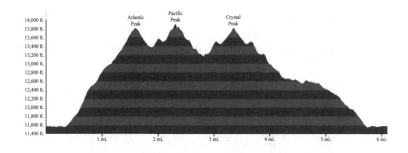

Overview This adventure demands good endurance, a bit of route-finding, and a good weather forecast. Do not be fooled by the low mileage and modest elevation gain—this is a big day, even for experienced mountain hikers. This route is the standard, but please read the "Notes" section on page 137 for details on some of the alternatives.

0.0 This route starts at the upper parking area. If you are parked at the lower parking lot, tack on 1.5 miles to walk up the road (though you may have an alternative hiking option around Mayflower Hill from this lot—read on to see more). The first 10 minutes of this hike are going to be soggy. Head north toward Atlantic's prominent west ridge. This involves about 200 feet of bashing through 7-foot-tall willows. While there is something of a trail through them, don't bother trying to find it—just find your way through. In the early morning, a rain shell is advised.

0.2 After clearing the willows, the slopes up to Atlantic's ridge are a welcome sight. A fairly well-worn trail appears and heads up Pacific Creek into the basin between Atlantic and Pacific—you'll be using it on the way back several hours from now. Head up through the grass-and-pine-tree slopes to the lower boulders of the ridge.

0.5 After a tough 0.5 mile, you are ready to line up Atlantic's west ridge. It's the best access line to these summits, consisting of solid rock and Class 2 scrambling. It has slight exposure near the top but otherwise is very straightforward. It's 1.0 mile to the top.

1.5 After a good push, reach the summit of Atlantic. Most summer days, a swarm of hikers can be seen atop Quandary Peak to the southeast. Pacific towers ahead to the north. The easiest descent to the saddle between the two is off the northeast slopes (the north ridge direct often has snow cover). The footing is good down to the saddle.

1.8 At 13,365 feet, the saddle between the two peaks is a good place to grab a snack. The lake just off to the north is Pacific Tarn at 13,420 feet. It is the highest elevation lake in the country whose name is recognized by the United States Board on Geographic Names. Neat. Onward to Pacific Peak.

2.3 The airy summit of Pacific Peak. The route to Crystal to the north looks imposing. Reaching the Pacific–Crystal ridge is the toughest part of your day and will involve some easy but exposed Class 3 downclimbing. From the summit, go back south and look for one of two short (30-foot) gullies that lead down into the deep notch just west of the summit. The first is about 80 feet from the summit and has black rock, thus the name "Black Gully." The second is about 50 feet past that and goes down and right (north) into the notch. Rock is solid in both places. Once in the notch, a short Class 3 scramble (slightly left of the notch) goes up to the far side of the notch. Views down into the notch gully are wild. Those who don't like exposure should keep their eyes up. After a small "almost" knife-edge, the boulders of the ridgeline appear. They are quite off camber at first but after about 100 feet ease off, and a hiker's trail appears down the ridge. The hardest part of your day is over. Enjoy the walk down to the saddle.

2.8 The low point of the saddle is at 13,184 feet. Continue north, staying slightly right of the main ridge for the best footing along a faint trail.

3.4 Crystal's hard-won summit! Two optional peaks are within striking distance here: Father Dyer Peak, 0.5 mile to the east, and Peak 10, 0.8 mile to the north. If you had to pick one, Father Dyer would be it. Not only is it shorter than Peak 10 (1.0 mile and 385 feet of elevation gain out and back), it's a tough peak to get from any other route—but it's a simple walk to get there via *this* route. Peak 10 has other good routes, but if you're feelin' it, it's 1.6 miles and 880 feet of elevation gain out and back from Pacific.

Head back down Crystal to Pacific–Crystal saddle.

3.9 You're back in the saddle again. This time, descend west down the boulder and begin the southwest walk back to Mayflower Gulch. There are no defined trails, but the boulder field is fairly stable, eventually yielding to firmer alpine fields. Note that if you parked at the lower, paved parking area, the quickest way back is to follow Humbug Creek back to the access road that passes under Mayflower Hill to the west. It's 3.7 miles from the saddle to the parking area from here.

If you're heading back to the upper parking area, continue southwest along rocky, grassy fields.

4.7 As you close in on the foot of the west ridge of Pacific Peak, stay high (left) and traverse through a boulder field with some big rocks. Some of these are not entirely stable, so test everything and aim for the grassy slopes on the high tail of the west ridge.

4.8 Now at the base of the west ridge, the basin walk eases up quite a bit. Begin heading down, eventually finding the Pacific Creek Trail. This is a better option than regaining the elevation at Atlantic's west ridge. The

High on Atlantic's superb west ridge

trail drops down, then turns right away from the creek and back into Mayflower Gulch.

5.8 Before calling it a day, you get to go one more round with the willows. Bash your way to a glorious finish!

6.1 Congratulations on completing an incredible traverse! Don't be surprised if a lot of day hikers are in the basin—it's a popular place, thanks to the interesting mining ruins.

Notes Here's a summary of a few options for these peaks:

Reverse Order

A good option if you're at the paved, lower parking. Start through the basin via Humbug Creek and up to the Pacific–Crystal saddle. Grab Crystal, then return to the saddle and up Pacific's north ridge. Then down and up to Atlantic and then down Atlantic's west ridge. You'll still have to mash through the willows, but you can kind of turn your brain off for the last 1.5 miles as you walk down the access road.

Atlantic–Pacific

If you want a shorter day, weather moves in, or you just can't stand Crystal Peak, this option is available. Returning back up and over Atlantic is one way. It's also possible to bail off the top of Pacific Peak's west ridge, though it involves a 1,000-foot scree-and-boulder mélange during the descent. Hike 0.2 mile down the west ridge. There will be some easy Class 3 downclimbs (stay right when in doubt). Reach a sandy, flat saddle. Beyond this, the west ridge gets difficult, so bail down the south slopes into the Pacific Creek Basin. It's loose but passable—if you are in a group, be careful not to knock rocks down on one another. Once you reach the basin, it's actually a pleasant walk back as the valley is festooned with wildflowers in the summertime.

Point-to-Point to Far East Trailhead

This route, 9.1 miles with 4,400 feet of elevation gain, starts the same as the trio all the way to Crystal. Thankfully, from Crystal on, the terrain eases up significantly. Hike over to Peak 10 (0.8 mile), then over to Peak 9 (0.6 mile) and down Peak 9 to the Wheeler Trail between Peaks 8 and 9. Follow the Wheeler Trail northwest to its junction with the Colorado Trail. Go left (west) and down to the Far East parking lot. Instead of three peaks, you get five. The traverse across Peaks 10 and 9 don't take long, and walking down the Colorado Trail is a treat. This is a very viable option since you pass the Far East Trailhead on the way to Mayflower Gulch and they are only about 7 miles apart (though there is the issue of the 1.5-mile four-wheel-drive road if you are using passenger cars).

One route that is not recommended is the Atlantic–Fletcher traverse. I have done the full Atlantic–Fletcher–Drift traverse, and it falls out of the scope of this guidebook, due to Class 4 (and possibly low Class 5) terrain on absolutely horrible rock. An alternative route to get to Fletcher Mountain (the highest thirteener in the Tenmile Range by 1 foot over Pacific) is presented on page 132.

30. ✪ Pacific Peak (13,950')–West Ridge

Round-Trip Distance	4.4 miles
Class	3+
Difficulty	9/10
Hiking Time	5.0–6.5 hours
Total Elevation Gain	2,800'
Terrain	Airy, exposed ridge on marginal rock, then descent down Atlantic Peak's solid west ridge. A helmet is advised.
Best Time to Climb	June–October

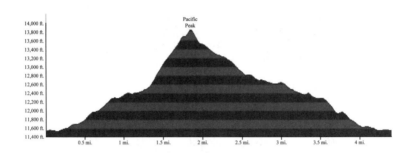

Overview To quote Tim the Enchanter from *Monty Python and the Holy Grail,* "If you do doubt your courage or your strength, come no further!" This exciting and challenging route toes the line between Class 3 and Class 4—but for those who enjoy a good scramble with exposure, it's an excellent line. It's more difficult than other Class 3 ridges in this book, such as Kelso Ridge and Pettingell Peak's east ridge. While the rock is loose in the lower section, thankfully it is more solid when you need it most along a short-lived knife-edge. The last portion of the ridge to the summit eases up considerably. One more thought: if the western Gore Range is on your hit list, this is an excellent preview of the typical terrain on those peaks.

Mile/Route **0.0** From the upper parking lot, follow the same initial line as you did for the Atlantic–Pacific–Crystal route: Bash west through the willows, then find the Pacific Creek access trail once you clear them. This time, however, rather than heading up to Atlantic's west ridge, stay on the access trail as it parallels Pacific Creek and into the basin. As you ascend, Pacific Peak's ridge will come into profile. Depart the trail and head north to the saddle between Mayflower Hill and Pacific Peak. Mayflower is a fun little add-on if you want to get a little extra credit (it's 0.2 mile from the saddle to the top of Mayflower Hill).

1.4 Behold, the mighty west ridge. A scrappy trail heads up through the boulders. Stay right of the first rock tower as the terrain gets steeper. After bypassing the tower to the right, stay close to its base on your left for the best footing. The next 0.3 mile presents the crux of the adventure.

As you bypass the end of the first rock tower, cross a gravel-encrusted gully to the right to reach more solid rock (don't go up the gully; better

Pacific Peak's trademark cracked summit as seen from the Pacific–Crystal saddle

rock is on the right). Ascend left to the ridgeline to what can be considered the second tower. The rock here is a little lighter in color. Scramble straight up this section, where the exposure markedly increases.

This is the crux of the route. Scramble along the ridge down to a small notch. Above this is a very narrow but very short knife-edge on solid rock. It's only about 10 feet long, but the exposure is big-time, enhanced by the exit off the knife-edge into a microsaddle that barely has standing room for one person. Past this, the rock quality improves. There are easier options off the ridge to the right as well. After following a natural line on the right, you'll be at a somewhat flat, sandy saddle at 13,330 feet. The hardest climbing is behind you. Note that this is the bail-out option down the south slopes as shown on the map (Class 2, loose but passable).

1.7 The going gets easier from here. From the saddle, a prow of rock blocks the ridge, and you can go left or right. Either works, but right has more solid rock—it's the way to go. After topping out the minigully on the right, the ridge reverts to a Class 2 walk all the way to Pacific's notch, which will present one final challenge.

1.9 At 13,780 feet, you'll encounter the deep notch that splits the west ridge and the summit. Luckily, this isn't as tricky as it may initially seem. Where the ridge ends at the notch, go right about 30 feet and find a good, solid downclimb into the south side of the notch saddle. Then, to hit the saddle, scramble up the "Black Gully," a 20-foot, enclosed gully that pops you out within spitting distance of the summit. There's also an option to go slightly right out of the notch and scramble up to the last portion of the south ridge.

2.0 Yahoo, the summit of Pacific Peak! The best way to get back is to drop down to Atlantic's north ridge, then return via Atlantic's west ridge (all Class 2) terrain. It's possible to use the bail-out line on Pacific, but it's a lousy route and should only be used if you are out of other options. So . . . onward to Atlantic.

2.4 The low point of the saddle. Continue up to Atlantic.

2.7 Atlantic's summit. Proceed down the west ridge. There will be a few easy, Class 2+ downclimbs.

3.7 At the bottom of Atlantic's west ridge, head south down the slopes back to Mayflower Gulch. There will be one more session of willow bashing to reach the upper parking area.

4.4 Done. And well done.

Notes   After topping out on Pacific, the options to head over to Crystal or the point-to-point to the Far East Trailhead described in the previous route are all good alternatives to the main route.

Pacific's west ridge can be climbed by going directly over the first tower, but that entails tough Class 4 climbing up and a low Class 5 downclimb of about 20 feet on the far side—and the rock isn't great. It's not advised, but experienced climbers may enjoy it.

31. ◌ Drift Peak (13,900')

Round-Trip Distance	3.0 miles
Class	2+
Difficulty	7/10
Hiking Time	5.0–6.5 hours
Total Elevation Gain	2,370'
Terrain	Loose, rocky slopes to solid ridge, then a boulder-strewn slope to finish.
Best Time to Climb	June–October

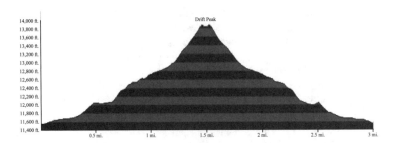

Overview   Yes, that meager mileage and mild elevation gain can take even strong climbers between 4 and 5 hours. Drift's northwest ridge (also informally called Villa Ridge) is organically broken up into three sections. It starts with a scrappy, gritty climb up the low shoulder, then follows a blissful ridge up to a conclusion of steep and mostly solid boulders.

Working up the lower section of Pacific Peak's west ridge (see page 138)

Mile/Route 0.0 From the upper parking, follow the remainder of the four-wheel-drive road up to Gold Hill. Your ridge will be in plain sight to the south, though the actual summit seems uncertain from this perspective.

0.4 This first push to the ridge has the worst rock of the day. It's loose, sandy, and boulders shift under your feet. A makeshift trail claws up right of the main ridge, but the better rock is to the left, close to the ridge proper. Stick to it until it flattens out.

0.7 Just like that, the ridge flattens out and improves significantly. The middle section of the ridge is a delight. A few pseudocatwalks (there's no real exposure) and old mining pits decorate the way. The steep finish on dark rock looms ahead.

1.2 After popping up through a bunny-ear notch, the last 800 vertical feet are waiting. It's only 0.3 mile, and there is something of a trail. The ridge itself angles slightly left—stay as centered on it as you can. The scrambling here isn't difficult, but it's sustained. Pace yourself.

1.5 After a big push, you'll see the summit plateau come into view. It's a short walk north over to the summit, which had a register in 2016. The fractured, disintegrating ridge north to Fletcher Mountain is a mess. However, if you want to grab it, read the "Notes" section on the next page. Otherwise, return the way you came. Take care on the initial downclimb, as well as the last slope, to reach the firm, grassy ground of Gold Hill.

3.0 Finish.

Notes Even for the adventurous, the ridges north and south off Fletcher Mountain are too rotten to be any fun, which is a shame because they look inviting from afar. If you do want to grab Fletcher from Drift, it is possible to keep the route at Class 3 (though note that the standard Class 2 up Fletcher is accessed from the upper Quandary Peak Trailhead to the east). It adds 2 miles round-trip and 1,100 feet of elevation gain. Descend off Drift north to a broad gully. This Class 3 downclimb leads to one of my personal favorite mountain plateaus in all of the Rocky Mountains. Roll over to the southeast ridge of Fletcher for an easy Class 2 walk-up. Return back to Drift the way you came.

The big ridge you see on Quandary is the Class 3 west ridge, a bona fide excellent line up this otherwise mellow fourteener—it's one of the best routes on any fourteener and compares to the standard route on another fourteener, Wilson Peak. It's a long way from Mayflower Gulch though—the Blue Lakes Trailhead from CO 9 via Forest Service Road 850 is the way to go (and probably the best way to get Fletcher as well).

Additional Route

Crystal Peak Direct

Class 2+ – 8 miles – 2,930' elevation gain

From the lower, paved parking, this is a good way to get Crystal Peak. Note that the standard route on Crystal is actually on the east side from Spruce Creek, but this is still a great route. I suggest pairing it up as a point-to-point with the Far East Trailhead at Copper Mountain for a great, unique day hike.

It's hard to tell on maps, but the four-wheel-drive road that splits left (north) off Mayflower Gulch's road is not passable by the public—it has a large concrete barrier. But it is a good walking trail. Follow it as it curves below Mayflower Hill into Humbug Creek Basin. The trail ends, so follow the slopes and meadows up to the Crystal–Pacific saddle and onward to Crystal Peak, 4.0 miles from the start.

If you want to grab Peak 10 and Peak 9 and do the point-to-point, it's 9.5 miles and 4,200 feet of elevation gain. This route has the advantage of following trails out to the Far East Trailhead versus the off-trail wandering needed to get back to Mayflower Gulch.

Copper Mountain/Spaulding Gulch Trailhead
(10,140')

Spaulding Gulch offers a unique adventure to this trio of peaks that has the added benefit of being entirely legal (certain routes to Jacque Peak from the south pass through private mining land; this one doesn't). Despite traversing through a developed ski area, Jacque Peak is a fun and challenging day hike—it was scenic enough to make the cover of this guide. Hiking up from Copper Village is fun as well. Taking a chairlift up is a lazy but novel way to get up to the ridgeline—the problem is that on most summer days, the lifts don't run until 10 a.m. (which is pushing it for storms). Maybe hoofing it is the best way to go.

PEAKS

- Copper Mountain: 12,441'
- Union Mountain: 12,313'
- Jacque Peak: 13,205'

Wilderness Area and Range

Arapaho National Forest, Copper Mountain/Gore Range

Trailhead Distance from I-70

Copper Mountain: 1.6 miles

Spaulding Gulch: 3.1 miles

Driving Directions

Copper Mountain: Take Exit 195 to CO 91S. Westbound, just go straight off the exit. Eastbound, it's right at the end of the exit. About 200 feet from the end of the exit, take a right at the light onto Copper Road and go 1.5 miles to the Beeler Lot in Copper Village. Summer parking is free at the Beeler Lot (as well as most other resort lots).

Spaulding Gulch: Take Exit 195 to CO 91S. Westbound, just go straight off the exit. Eastbound, it's right at the end of the exit. At the lighted intersection with Copper Road/Conoco, reset your odometer. It's very easy to miss the turnoff for Spaulding—it's not marked or designated. Go 2.5 miles along CO 91S. Before Fremont Pass starts climbing, there is a turnoff on the right side of the road. If you reach the mine area tailing ponds on the right, you've gone too far.

At the gravel pulloff, an unexpected dirt road goes up a short hill (about 0.2 mile) to some nice car camping spots for four-wheel drives or SUVs. Passenger cars will park just off CO 91S in the lower gravel lot. When you pull out to head home, **do not attempt to take a left out of the lot.** Take a right and turn around a bit farther up the road where visibility of oncoming traffic is better. Attempting a left is asking for trouble.

Vehicle Recommendations

Any vehicle can make either trailhead, though passenger cars won't be able to safely make it up the few hundred feet at the base of Spaulding

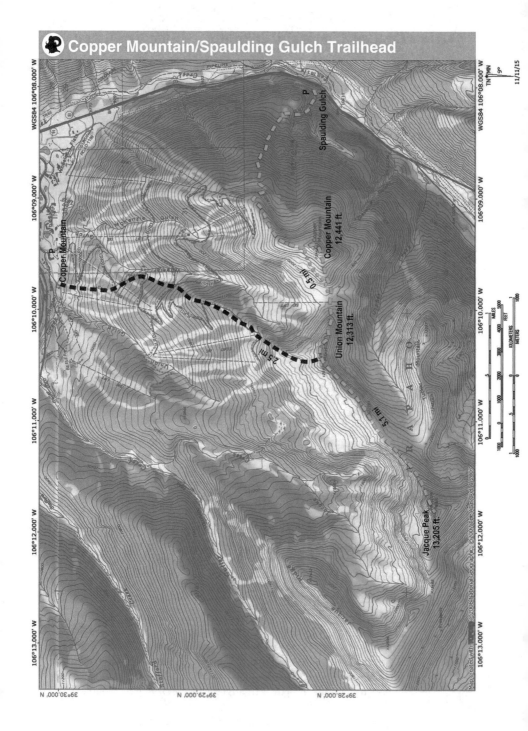

Copper Mountain/Spaulding Gulch Trailhead

Copper Mountain
12,441 ft.

Spaulding Gulch

Union Mountain
12,313 ft.

0.5 mi

2.5 mi

5.1 mi

Jacque Peak
13,205 ft.

WGS84 106°08.000' W

106°09.000' W

106°10.000' W

106°11.000' W

106°12.000' W

106°13.000' W

N 39°30.000'

N 39°29.000'

N 39°28.000'

TN MN 9°

11/11/15

Gulch. SUVs and SUCs can muscle up the short hill as long as they have decent clearance.

Fees/Camping There are no fees to hike or camp here—unless you want to take the chairlift up.

Dog Regulations Dogs are allowed under voice control or on leash. Please leash up your pup at Copper Village.

Summary Count me among the hikers who spent far too long avoiding summer hikes at ski areas. Jacque Peak has obvious appeal, thanks to the stunning profile it cuts from below. However, both Copper and Union Mountains prove to be interesting little summits as well. The Spaulding Gulch access is a unique passage that enhances the ghost town feel of an empty ski resort (not to mention avoiding trespassing on mining territory).

Primary Routes

32. ✪ Jacque Peak (13,205') via Spaulding Gulch

Round-Trip Distance	9.4 miles
Class	2
Difficulty	7/10
Hiking Time	6–8 hours
Total Elevation Gain	4,260'
Terrain	Steep hills on ski resort to rolling ridges leading to solid boulder field to Jacque Peak.
Best Time to Climb	June–October. Note that once ski operations begin in November, this route is closed until ski season's end (usually the first two weeks of April).

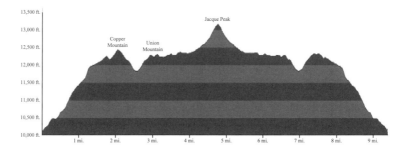

Overview It's worth taking a look at the start of this hike on Google Maps or Google Earth—it's a tricky start (see the photo on page 147). The approach to the ski area heads up a long-overgrown access road. Now thick with grass and wildflowers, this peaceful corridor is a nice intro to a big day. Once you hit the ski hills at the base of the Resolution Lift, get ready for some steep

The namesake mountain of the ski area, Copper Mountain

hiking—though it'll be a beautiful grind as you push onwards through wildflowers. Atop the Resolution Lift, the traverse begins and the views open up. Hiking poles and gaiters are a grand idea—the morning grass is usually soaked with dew and can be slick in places.

A two-vehicle point-to-point is easy to set up and is a nice option—hike down to Copper Village and enjoy a cold one after your adventure. This spares the steep descent down the Resolution Lift as well as having to regain Copper Mountain's summit.

Mile/Route **0.0** From the cluster of parking spots along the dirt road, head uphill to a grassy meadow. There are two paths: one left, one right. The correct one is the grassy meadow to the left (the right is a 0.2-mile walk-up to old mine ruins). Head to the grassy opening where a wide corridor follows a small creek for a short time. Faint access trails appear in the tall grass. Follow the corridor upward.

0.5 At the top of the corridor, the woods open up to reveal the lower towers of the Resolution Lift. There are no trails, but the wide-open slopes are easy to follow. Stay under Resolution (on what will be the Highline Trail come winter). Your heart will be pumping.

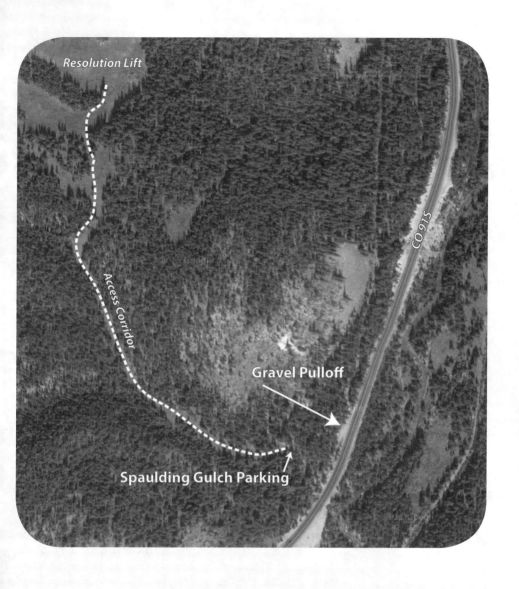

Resolution Lift

Access Corridor

CO 91S

Gravel Pulloff

Spaulding Gulch Parking

1.0 Heading into the trees to the right of the open swath provides a bit of shade and better footing. Plus it's pretty in the early morning light. A few streams trickle through the pines. Continue up.

1.2 A snowcat road intersects the hill. You can see the top of the Resolution Lift, but it looks like a steep bugger to go directly up to. The easiest way up is to go into the woods to the left of the road for about 300 feet, then start up the slope there. Going farther left brings you into Spaulding Bowl, which is just as steep. Buck up and make the 370-vertical-foot push to the top of the lift and into the developed ski area.

1.6 The great ridge walk begins. Copper Mountain to the southwest is the first goal. Pass a few buildings and walk up the rim of Spaulding Bowl on a trail that happens to head up to Copper Mountain. The Storm King Lift ends just prior to the summit of Copper Mountain.

2.2 The summit of Copper. Head west to Union Mountain down steep slopes. There's a nice little lake for you/your dog to soak your feet/paws in the saddle between the two mountains. Navigation is easy, as this section is developed. Continue up to Union Mountain.

3.3 The summit of Union Mountain and the top of the Black Jack Lift. The woods in this area are tastefully named Fremont Glades. Carry on the rolling ridge toward Jacque Peak, now looking larger than ever.

4.5 After a relatively flat traverse, the ski boundaries end and the climb up the east ridge of Jacque begins at 12,470 feet. The ridge boulder fields are solid, and intermittent hiking trails appear. The views northwest toward Vail Pass are amazing. Stay on the ridge or just below on the left side for the best footing.

4.8 Just below the summit is a small rock outcrop that requires easy scrambling to get over. Alternatives to the left exist but add on a few hundred feet of extra work.

The rocky scramble near the summit of Jacque

5.1 The incredible summit of Jacque Peak. The Tenmile Range to the east and the Gores and Sawatch Peaks to the west make Jacque feel like the centerpiece of the amazing array of mountains.

If you wish to return the way you came to Spaulding Gulch, you'll have to regain Union Mountain and Copper Mountain. Union is no big deal, but Copper is some work. Descending the ski mountain via the Ottobahn Trail, down Rendezvous Lift, and down below the American Flyer Lift is the easiest way to reach the village.

If you are returning the way you came, you'll regain Union Mountain around 6.7 miles, then chug up Copper Mountain (bypassing a bit to the left to avoid extra elevation gain) around mile 7.8. The access trail will go down to the Resolution Lift, where a steep descent awaits (it does go by rather quickly).

9.2 Finally, the bottom of the Resolution Lift! Follow the Spaulding Gulch corridor back to the parking area.

Notes   Hiking up from Copper Village may be more developed, but it's still a fun hike. If you get an early start, you'll likely have most of the mountain to yourself (at least on the way up). If you want to get all three peaks, stay under (or near) American Eagle Lift, then Excelsior Lift. This will bring you to the building below Copper Mountain itself and then follow the route description from there. If just Jacque Peak is your goal, go American Flyer to Sierra to Mountain Chief and gain Jacque's east ridge.

Just because this is a developed area, don't be lazy—start early (6 a.m. at the latest). Adding a mountain bike into the equation from Copper Village is an option, at least to get to the start of ridgeline. The Colorado Trail passes under and around Jacque Peak to Searle Pass, which can be used to gain the west ridge of Jacque Peak. Not a practical day hike, but if you happen to be a peak bagger along the Colorado Trail, it's one way to score this well-named thirteener.

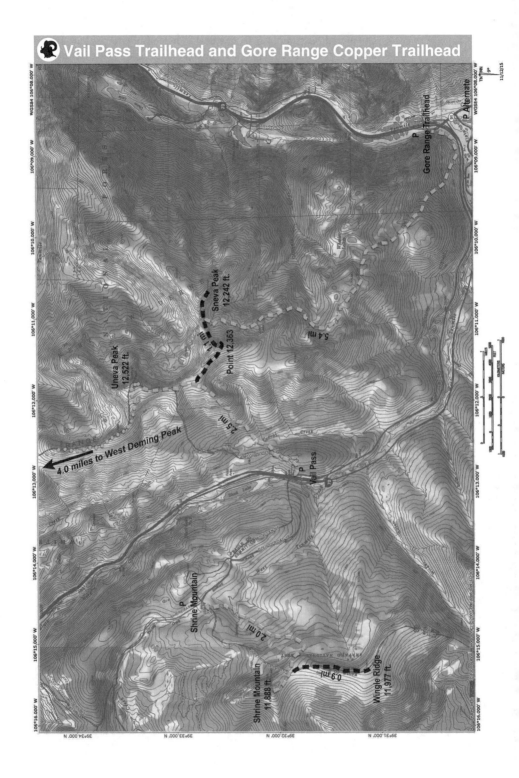

Vail Pass Trailhead and Gore Range Copper Trailhead

Gore Range Trailhead

P Alternate

P

5.4 mi

Sneva Peak
12,242 ft.

Point 12,363

2.5 mi

Uneva Peak
12,522 ft.

4.0 miles to West Deming Peak

P Vail Pass

Shrine Mountain

P

2.0 mi

Shrine Mountain
11,888 ft.

0.9 mi

Wingle Ridge
11,977 ft.

Vail Pass Trailhead (10,662') and Gore Range Copper Trailhead (9,680')

These peaks represent the last of the "easy" Gore Range summits. All Class 2 hikes, there are a few ways to approach these adventures. If you're looking for a quick outing, Uneva Peak off Vail Pass will do the job. If you want to soak in the deep beauty of the Gore Range Trail and the photogenic Wheeler Lakes (and want a longer day out), go for the Gore Range Trail. Shrine Mountain and Wingle Ridge have great views of one of Colorado's most recognizable mountains, Mount of the Holy Cross in the Sawatch Range. For pure hiking, this area is spot on.

PEAKS

- Shrine Mountain: 11,888'
- Wingle Ridge: 11,977'
- Uneva Peak: 12,522'
- Sneva Peak: 12,242'
- Point 12,363: 12,363'
- West Deming Peak: 12,736'

Wilderness Area and Range

White River National Forest, Arapaho National Forest, Eagles Nest Wilderness, Gore Range

Trailhead Distance from I-70

Vail Pass: Directly off highway exit for Uneva Peak. Shrine Pass Parking is 2.4 miles from the pass.

Gore Range Trailhead: Park either directly off Exit 195 or at Copper Mountain's Alpine Lot and walk over the pedestrian bridge to the Gore Range Trail.

Driving Directions

Vail Pass: For the Uneva Peak direct route, take Exit 190. If coming west-bound, pull off to the right at the end of the exit and park on the side of the road. Eastbound, take a left off the exit then a left once over the bridge to reach the same spot. For Shrine Mountain Parking, take Exit 190. West-bound, go left off the exit, eastbound right. The dirt Shrine Mountain Road is on the right. Follow it 2.4 miles to the parking lot.

Gore Range: If coming westbound, take Exit 195. A few hundred feet along the highway ramp on the right side of the road are spots to park for about 200 feet. If this area is full, continue onto Copper Mountain Alpine Lot parking. Go straight at the light at the end of the exit, and in about 150 feet, pull right into the Alpine Lot. (Parking is free in the summer unless Copper Mountain is hosting an event. Call ahead at 970-968-2318.) If all that doesn't work, you can park in the scenic viewing area, which is only accessible from westbound I-70. It's the pulloff after passing Officers Gulch (Exit 198) that borders some tailing ponds. Gore Range Trail passes through here. Head south on it if you park here.

Eastbound, it's easiest to take Exit 195, go right at the end of the ramp, and park in the Alpine Lot. If it's not open, take Exit 198 (Officers Gulch) and get back on I-70 westbound and park in the scenic pulloff lot mentioned above.

Vehicle Recommendations Any car can make these trailheads. The Shrine Pass Road is well-maintained dirt but is passable to the trailhead by all cars unless there is snow.

Fees/Camping There are no fees to hike or camp here in the summer, but November–May there is a $6 day-use fee to park at Vail Pass. Dispersed camping is allowed along the Shrine Pass Road. The Shrine Mountain Inn cabins are also available to rent from the 10th Mountain Division (huts.org for more info).

Dog Regulations Dogs are allowed under voice control or on leash.

Summary Long days in the mountains on great trails in a beautiful setting—what more could a hiker ask for? These walk-up summits stand in mellow contrast to the bulk of Gore Range peaks, which require strong navigational skills and technical climbing.

Primary Routes

33. ✪ Uneva Peak Direct (12,522')

Round-Trip Distance	**5 miles**
Class	**2**
Difficulty	**4/10**
Hiking Time	**4–6 hours**
Total Elevation Gain	**2,040'**
Terrain	**Easy off-trail slopes.**
Best Time to Climb	**June–September**

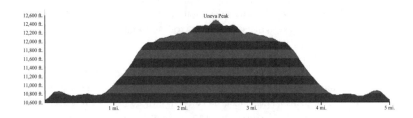

Overview Uneva Peak Direct takes advantage of sparsely wooded forests and a high starting elevation. As an out-and-back, it's a nice day out, but if you want to get more out of it, consider adding on Sneva Peak and Point 12,363 and descending via the Gore Range Trail by Wheeler Lakes. This is an easy point-to-point to set up and covers a lot of ground without a lot of effort (the tour back to the Gore Range Trailhead is all downhill).

photographed by Wendy Cranford

Uneva Peak as seen from Shrine Pass

Mile/Route **0.0** From the Vail Pass parking directly off the right of Exit 195, take the access trails up through the woods. These trails lead to Corral Creek drainage, the first part of your day. The views open up as you near the creek.
0.7 Rather than take the trail along the creek, head northeast up the broad slopes between Uneva Peak and Point 12,363. The slopes can be a little steep in places, so poles help. Carry on to the ridge.
1.8 At 12,100 feet, you stand atop the flat saddle south of Uneva Peak. It's the biggest thing around . . . so get moving! You're almost there. The south ridge has a hiker's trail to Uneva's summit.
2.5 Atop Uneva Peak! You can return the way you came for a solid 5-mile day. Or . . . if you are looking for more, read the "Notes" below. Otherwise, go back the way you came.
5.0 Finish.

Notes There are two extra-credit options—the point-to-point south to the Gore Range Trailhead (grabbing Sneva Peak and Point 12,363; more on this route in a moment) or the long traverse over to West Deming Peak (see bonus map on the next page). It's a 13.1-mile out-and-back from Vail Pass and over 5,600 feet of elevation gain, but that said, the walk on the rolling ridges from Uneva to West Deming is gorgeous—and you'll have the place to yourself. It's a big day, but fit hikers can reasonably do it in good time (it took me 7.5 hours).

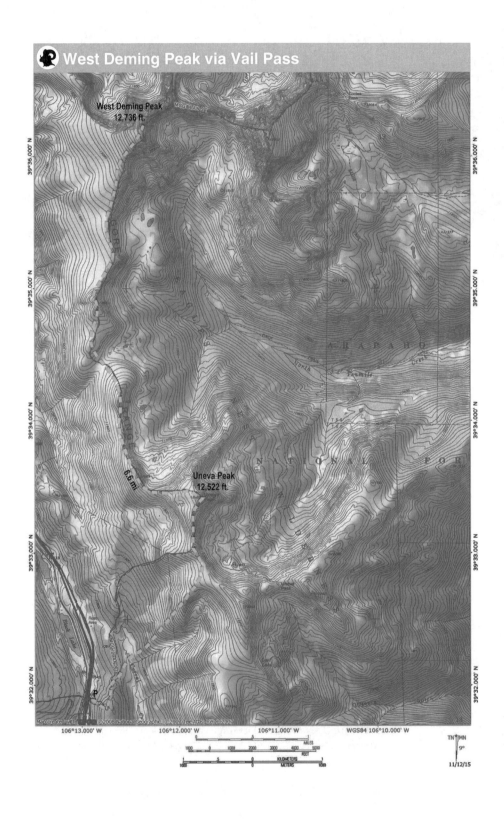

West Deming Peak via Vail Pass

West Deming Peak
12,736 ft.

Uneva Peak
12,522 ft

6.6 mi

P

The point-to-point to the Gore Range Trailhead can be done either way, but starting at Vail Pass is easier since you only gain 2,570 feet but drop 3,540 feet. Switch those elevation gains if you start at the Gore Range Trailhead. Once you get Uneva, go south to the saddle again, and this time go east down to Uneva Pass and the Gore Range Trail. From Uneva Pass, Point 12,363 is 0.2 mile away (if you didn't take it to reach the pass) and Sneva is 0.3 mile away—nice, quick side trips. From there it's about 5.4 miles south down the Gore Range Trail to the parking areas. Total mileage is about 8.5 miles, depending on how directly you took the way up to Uneva Peak.

34. ✪ Shrine Mountain (11,888') and Wingle Ridge (11,977')

Round-Trip Distance	5.7 miles
Class	1/2
Difficulty	2/10
Hiking Time	3–5 hours
Total Elevation Gain	1,210'
Terrain	Well-worn trail to easy, off-trail ridge walk.
Best Time to Climb	June–September

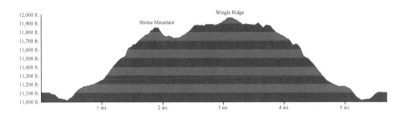

Overview One of the easier days out (for this guide), this is still a scenic and enjoyable hike. Shrine Mountain is actually a subsummit of Wingle Ridge, its parent peak, despite the unpeaklike name. There are very good views of the Tenmile Range, including Pacific Peak, and the Sawatch Range, including Mount of the Holy Cross.

Mile/Route 0.0 From the Shrine Mountain parking lot, take the trail southwest to the ridge between Shrine Mountain and Wingle Ridge. It splits from the road to Shrine Mountain Inn a few feet in. Head to the ridge.
1.7 At the flat saddle, you go north for Shrine Mountain, south for Wingle Ridge. Let's go to Shrine Mountain first.
2.0 Shrine Mountain. Huzzah! Now, south to Wingle Ridge. Carry on past the saddle to the high point of the ridge.
3.3 The highest point of Wingle Ridge is 11,977 feet. It doesn't have the trees that Shrine Mountain does, so the views are better—and quite nice. From here, head back to the saddle and take the trail to the parking lot.
5.7 Finish.

Notes This is a popular area in the winter for skiers and snowshoers. Even though the peaks are not high, there is still an avalanche risk.

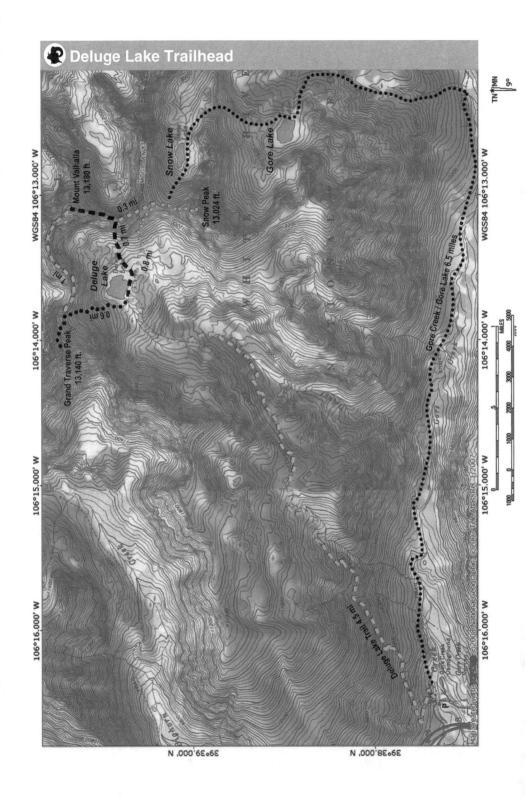

Deluge Lake Trailhead

XX. Deluge Lake Trailhead (8,720')

The peaks surrounding Deluge Lake are Colorado masterpieces. For those who love exploring rugged terrain tinged with a bit of danger, these are your mountains. Mount Valhalla's west face is a matrix of secret corridors but, with the correct route-finding, can be kept at Class 3. Grand Traverse is a blunt fellow, simply challenging all comers to grind up its steep Class 2 slopes. And Snow Peak is the absolute gem of this area—if you only get one summit, this is it. A good, tough Class 3 scramble awaits. It's possible to link all three together in a day. It's highly suggested to camp out at Deluge Lake the night before your summit attempts.

PEAKS

- Grand Traverse Peak: 13,140'
- Snow Peak: 13,024'
- Mount Valhalla: 13,180'

Wilderness Area and Range

White River National Forest, Eagles Nest Wilderness, Gore Range

Trailhead Distance from I-70

2.5 miles

Driving Directions

Take Exit 180. Westbound, go left off the exit and under the I-70 bridge and stay straight through the intersection. This will put you on Big Horn Road as it bends left. Eastbound, simply take a right off the exit and you'll be on Big Horn Road. Go east on Big Horn Road 2 miles, passing under I-70 one more time. The Deluge Lake Trailhead parking will be on your left. The Gore Creek Campground (paid) is here as well. A few hundred feet past the trailhead, the road ends and turns into the Vail Bike Path.

Vehicle Recommendations   Any vehicle can make it to the trailhead.

Fees/Camping   There are no fees to camp or hike in this area. The Gore Creek Campground is $20/night. On the west side of the road is a small, free pocket of dispersed campsites.

Dog Regulations   Dogs are allowed on leash in the Eagles Nest Wilderness. *Note:* As someone who loves hiking with his dogs, I actually prefer to leave them behind on this adventure. This area is very pristine, and there is an abundance of wildlife, especially mountain goats.

Summary   The Deluge Lake area makes for a glorious weekend of backpacking, camping, and summit scrambles. Just hiking to the lake area has summitlike stats: 4.5 miles one way and 3,200 feet of elevation gain. Camping up here is not only beautiful, it helps you get an early start in the morning to grab the summits before storms roll in. These summits are possible as day hikes of course, but aim for a predawn start.

Primary Routes

35. ✪ Deluge Lake Summits Tour

Round-Trip Distance	Varies; it is 9.0 miles from the trailhead to Deluge Lake and back (4.5 miles one way). See the following "Mile/Route" descriptions for mileages to the peaks.
Class	3+
Difficulty	10/10
Hiking Time	2 days; or expect 9–11 hours for a day hike. Summits are 3–5 hours from Deluge Lake; give 4–6 hours for full Grand Traverse–Snow traverse.
Total Elevation Gain	Varies; see above. Elevation to Deluge Lake is 3,200'.
Terrain	Well-traveled, Class 2 trail to Deluge Lake. Peaks are steep, loose in places, with rock gullies, boulders, and off-camber grass ramps. Bring a helmet. Strong route-finding skills are required for Valhalla Peak and the traverses between summits; Grand Traverse Peak and Snow Peak are more straightforward and easy to navigate.
Best Time to Climb	June–September

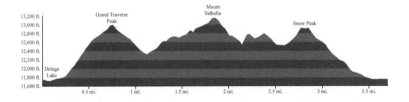

Overview Hail to the adventurous, your time has come! It is an interesting coincidence that as I-70 rolls west the peaks get progressively more difficult. If you've dialed in the Front Range and attempted the Tenmile Range, you're ready for the Gores. Snow Peak is arguably the best single-summit option here, thanks to its excellent Class 3 scramble along the north ridge. Valhalla is an exciting, route-finding adventure for those who love unlocking the secrets in a mountain's face (and one of my personal favorite routes in Colorado). Grand Traverse is a big hunk of rock that entails a steep, sustained Class 2 walk-up—if there's one peak that can be eschewed, it's Grand Traverse. The ridge walk connecting them all is exciting, especially from Valhalla to Snow Peak. And if all that doesn't entice you, simply camping at the lake is quite nice as well.

Deluge Lake as seen from the traverse between Valhalla and Snow Peaks

Mile/Route 0.0 From the busy parking lot, head off toward the well-signed Deluge Lake/Gore Creek Trail. In a few hundred feet is a signed split for Gore Greek/Deluge Lake. Switchback left (west) onto the Deluge Lake Trail. From there, it's a solid, easy-to-follow trail all the way to the lake. Pass a few boulder fields and steep hills and eventually reach the high basin.
4.0 After a long trek through the forest, you'll drop down into a wide-open basin below the lake. These last pine and shrub groves are good places to camp. You can also go up to the lake and pitch your tent in the trees south or east of the lake itself. It is advised to camp in the shelter of trees as the winds can blow with authority along the open tundra. Note there is an old cabin due south of the lake.
4.5 Deluge Lake. Because mileage will vary, depending on your summits, each route will be broken down from here. Reset your odometer to zero at the lake.

Grand Traverse Peak Direct:

- 1.3 miles round-trip to Deluge Lake (10.3 miles full round-trip)
- 1,200' elevation gain; Class 2

There's nothing subtle about this route. See big rock. Walk up big rock. It's only about 0.6 mile up the southeast slopes. The grassy/rocky footing is acceptable but not great. It's easiest to aim left of the low saddle between Grand Traverse Peak and Point 12,670 and stay on the slopes. Grind your way to a summit with fantastic views (and if you're feeling it, the start of the full three-peak traverse).

Mount Valhalla Direct:

- 1.6 miles round-trip to Deluge Lake (10.6 miles full round-trip)
- 1,410' elevation gain; Class 3

The west face of Valhalla has a lot of exciting options. It will take good route-finding and a little exploring to the top, but it's a lot of fun. The rock is loose, especially on the lower flanks, so bring a helmet for this one. It can be tricky to describe these routes (remember you can download the GPX tracks at mountainouswords.com/I70-hikes).

Looking at the west face from Deluge Lake, you'll see a high, prominent point south of Valhalla's summit, to the right of a craggy saddle. I'll refer to this formation as the Valhalla Shield. Directly below is a rocky face that, about halfway down the mountain, turns into the "Scree V"—a band of solid rock splits the scree, making it look like the letter V (fitting for Mount "Valhalla"). There are also prominent grassy slopes left of the scree field that go up to the ridgeline/saddle.

There are two main options. Both start by heading up the scree slopes, aiming for the top of the rock band that splits the slope in a V. From there, the more tame (and less exciting) route is to traverse the steep scree over to the equally steep grass slopes, then claw your way up to the saddle, then left (north) up to Valhalla's summit. Even if you are just hiking Valhalla, this is a crummy but possible direct way down. A better descent is from the Valhalla–Snow saddle. Read on for those details.

The other option will make you feel like a visitor in the halls of the mountain kings. At the top of the rock band at the Scree V, a hidden gully reveals itself. Shaded by the rock, this incredible passage aims to bring you to the base of the Valhalla Shield. Head up into it, where the rock gets more solid—and likely colder, since the sun is blocked. Stay right—you will pass a tempting, boulder-choked gully on your left that looks promising—it's not. It fizzles out in a short distance (and it's difficult to scramble up past the large, low boulder at the base).

Continue scrambling up right after this spot, then begin to trend a bit left. Eventually you'll see the impressive wall of rock that makes up the shield. Scramble up gravelly rock up a ramp to the left, eventually topping out in the morning light on the high ridge. For a moment it looks like your adventure may be foiled—the ridge cliffs out! However, if you go left (west) about 100 feet, a grassy/rocky passage is a welcome site. It's an easy downclimb to the flat, easy final slopes to the summit of Valhalla. Once you've won the saddle, it's 0.2 mile north to the top.

Now . . . how to get down? Return via the grassy ramps is one option, but they are steep and unpleasant and can be dangerously slick. More fun is to return to the base of the shield and head up and right back to the ridge (bypassing the shield feature). From the base of the shield, the route to follow is a steep, solid Class 3 line. Note that there is an interesting rock slab ramp in view to the south. Don't be tempted to traverse there; the better rock is a more direct line to the ridge. The scrambling at this point is very good. You will top out through a small notch to the right (south) of the shield. If you're the gutsy type, it's a Class 4, highly exposed scramble about 60 feet from here to the high point on the shield, about 12,770 feet—it's 100% optional.

Once you've gained the ridge, simply traverse south, staying to the right of the rock towers, and the path down to the saddle between Valhalla and Snow will come into view. You don't have to make the saddle (unless you want to tack on Snow Peak). Begin descending the steep, grassy slopes, where a few hiker's trails begin to materialize. Follow them down, through a boulder field, and back to the lake.

Valhalla–Snow Traverse:

- 2.4 miles round-trip to Deluge Lake (11.4 miles full round-trip)
- 2,010' elevation gain, Class 3+

Read the Valhalla Direct route above. Now, rather than descend before the Valhalla–Snow saddle, head up to it then continue south along Snow Peak's excellent south ridge. The scrambling here is delightful and solid—and there is even something of a trail. The best line curls a bit left just before topping out. Summit Snow and return to Deluge Lake from the saddle.

Snow Peak Direct:

- 1.8 miles round-trip to Deluge Lake (10.8 miles full round-trip)
- 1,200' elevation gain, Class 3

In contrast to Valhalla, this is a very direct route. From Deluge Lake, aim toward the low saddle between Valhalla and Snow. The lower part of these slopes requires navigation through a burly boulder field. Luckily, most of the rock is solid. Above the boulders, the grassy slopes offer a few improvised trails to the saddle. From there, hit the south ridge and enjoy fantastic scrambling 0.3 mile to the top. Return the way you came.

Grand Traverse–Valhalla Traverse:

- 2.5 miles round-trip to Deluge Lake (11.5 miles full round-trip)
- 2,100' elevation gain; Class 3+

Probably the worst combo route in this area, since the way up is a grind and the way down is on loose, steep slopes. However, the traverse between the two is a hoot. Get up Grand Traverse, then head east. It's roughly 1 mile between Grand Traverse and Valhalla Peak along the connecting ridge. The terrain is solid rock with good scrambles. There are a few notches to downclimb, which are generally easier on the left side. Good route-finding will help you avoid Class 4 territory. Once you top Valhalla, the grassy slopes on the west face are the most logical way down . . . however, it's better to just continue to the Valhalla–Snow saddle (see previous page) for a descent. And of course if you're going that far, why not get up Snow Peak too? See below.

Grand Traverse–Valhalla–Snow Traverse:

- 3.7 miles round-trip to Deluge Lake (12.7 miles full round-trip)
- 2,870' elevation gain; Class 3+

The full amphitheater tour. Outside of the initial work to get up Grand Traverse Peak, the rest of this route is a scrambler's dream. Class 4 looms in many places, but read the routes described above to find the best lines. Make sure you have a safe weather forecast, especially for the time you'll be between Grand Traverse and the saddle of Valhalla–Snow. It's truly no-man's-land.

Notes   The nameless peaks to the southwest of Grand Traverse Peak are actually pretty fun, Class 3 scrambles. The mantra to remember on all these peaks is "there's always a Class 3 option"—and there is. Be patient and take your time to figure out the safest, most solid lines.

Additional Route

Gore Lake to Snow Peak

Class 3 – 13 miles round-trip – 4,450' elevation gain

This is an interesting overnight option (or a very long day hike). Rather than turn off to Deluge Lake at the very start of the hike, go straight on the Gore Creek Trail. Four miles in along this gradually inclined trail, you'll reach the split for Gore Lake at the humble grave of two brothers, Andrew and Daniel Recen, early settlers in the area. Take the Gore Lake Trail to Gore Lake (5.4 miles), a good place to set up camp if you want to do this as a two-day adventure. Head up and right of Snow Peak's craggy east ridge up to Snow Lake. Head up to the saddle. Be careful if you plan to leave your backpacks here while you make the Snow Peak summit run; the goats and marmots are very curious. Tag Snow Peak (7.0 miles) then return via the Deluge Lake Trail for a big loop.

Extra Credit

One of the very best weekend backpacking trips is a point-to-point from the Meadow Creek Trailhead in Frisco to Deluge Lake Trailhead via the Gore Range Trail. Because it doesn't naturally grab any summits, it's not a featured route. See the Meadow Creek Trailhead chapter (see page 111) to start this route. Head up the Meadow Creek Trail, up and over Eccles Pass, and then up and over Red Buffalo Pass and head west along the Gore Creek Trail. It's a 12- to 14-mile route (depending how you approach Red Buffalo Pass) and can be the foundation for a good few days of peak bagging and backpacking.

Pitkin Creek Trailhead (8,480')

*This four-pack of peaks offers an airy, peaceful ridge walk after quite a bit
of work to get up there. Despite the off-trail nature of the route, none of these
peaks ever get over Class 2+ in technical difficulty. The trick here is finding
the best place to leave the well-manicured Pitkin Creek Trail and find your
way into the basin below Mount Solitude. After that, it's a straight-up hike
on slopes that are solid but peppered with slick rocks. Mount Solitude is the
featured attraction, but since you're up here . . . why not add on a few other
summits? You'll be forgiven if you opt out of Climbers Point's precariously bal-
anced summit boulder.*

PEAKS

- Mount Solitude: 13,090'
- Vista Peak: 13,075'
- Climbers Point: 13,005'
- Skiers Point: 12,620'

Wilderness Area and Range

White River National Forest, Eagles Nest Wilderness, Gore Range

Trailhead Distance from I-70

0.3 mile

Driving Directions

Take Exit 180 on I-70. Westbound, take a right off the exit then a quick
right onto North Frontage Road. Follow it 0.2 mile to the Pitkin Creek
Trailhead, which is about 100 feet from a condo complex. Please park in the
designated area.

For eastbound, go left off the exit, under the bridge, and past the
westbound exit to North Frontage Road and go right.

Vehicle Recommendations

Any vehicle can make this trailhead.

Fees/Camping

There are no fees to hike or camp in this area.

Dog Regulations

Dogs are allowed on leash only in the Eagles Nest Wilderness.

Summary

These Gore Range Peaks never encounter technical terrain, but the off-trail
terrain required to reach them will take some literal bushwhacking. There
are 3.5 miles of established trails before the real fun begins. Crash through
a thicket of trees and bushes before emerging in a stunningly serene basin.
From here, steep slopes will test your endurance as you push up to the
ridgelines. Once atop Mount Solitude, touring the ridgeline is a special
treat—views are great, and the walking is easy. Return the way you came or
from other similar steep slopes off Vista Peak.

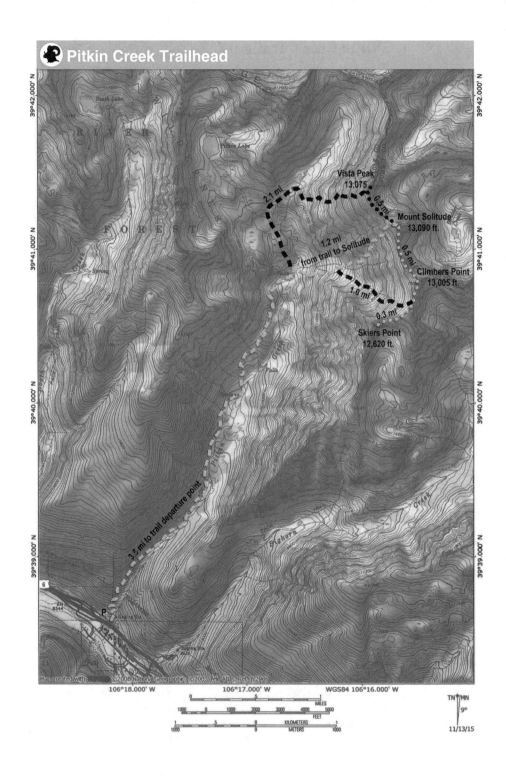

Vista Peak
13,075

2.1 mi

0.5 mi

Mount Solitude
13,090 ft.

1.2 mi
from trail to Solitude

0.5 mi

Climbers Point
13,005 ft.

1.0 mi

0.3 mi

Skiers Point
12,620 ft.

3.5 mi to trail departure point

P

Primary Routes

36. ✪ Mount Solitude (13,090') and Climbers Point (13,005') Tour

Round-Trip Distance	10.8 miles
Class	2+
Difficulty	8/10
Hiking Time	6–9 hours
Total Elevation Gain	4,850'
Terrain	Excellent trail to off-trail bushwhacking and steep slope hike on mixed grass/embedded rock hills. Poles are a good idea.
Best Time to Climb	June–October

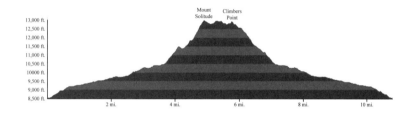

Overview   The total of 7 miles up and down on the Pitkin Creek Trail will go by relatively quickly; the 2.4 miles you'll spend off-trail may take just as long! There are a few different options to get up and down, and they are all steep. Navigation isn't overly difficult, and the bushwhacking can be fun if you're into that sort of thing. This is a lush area with many tributary creeks, waterfalls, and lakes. It's a big day hike or a nice option for a two-day adventure.

Mile/Route   0.0   From the civilized trailhead, cross a wooden bridge and head up along the Pitkin Creek Trail toward Pitkin Lake. This is a wonderful way to start the day—the trail isn't too steep, but it gains ground in good time. The aspen and pine forests are especially beautiful in autumn. Enjoy the waterfalls you'll see along the way.

3.1   If you're thinking of camping, this is a good place to start looking for a spot.

3.5   After passing through a brief, swampy section of trail (and past the impressive waterfall off to the right of the trail), you'll start to head up the west side of the sloping valley wall. The Solitude Basin will be up and off to your right. Where the trail hits a low point before climbing, head off the trail to the right and toward the basin.

Before you reach the main, open basin, there's some bushwhacking to do. There's no obvious line, but after trying them all, my advice is to stay far right of the waterfall that splits the basin, sticking to the pine trees rather than the willows and bushes. This is the best footing and avoids getting drenched by soggy branches and towering willows. There's no trick here; just keep bashing up to the open basin. It's not far away.

3.8 After fighting through the foliage, the open basin is yours. Climbers Point is right of the center of the basin, Solitude left. Skiers Point's craggy ridge extends to the right (south). The easiest way up is likely the direct line to the saddle between Climbers Point and Skiers Point—but only slightly easier. For Mount Solitude, the middle of its west slope is the best line. Going too far left offers the same terrain but adds distance. There are a few stray pockets of pine trees halfway up, then it's a straight grind to the summit—just under a mile away.

4.7 Finally, Mount Solitude! Climbers Point is an easy 0.5 mile south of the summit, and Skiers Point is 0.3 mile past that. The easiest way back down to the basin and eventually the trail is via the west slopes between Climbers and Skiers Points. So in other words, at least go up and over Climbers Point to get back down. The summit boulder on Climbers Point is wild—it is perched over the eastern void, looking as if it could tumble down at any second. If you hop on it for your summit photo . . . don't linger.

7.3 Get down through the basin, fumble through the forested slopes (now on your left) and regain the Pitkin Creek Trail. It's an easy walk out from here . . . enjoy it!

10.8 Finish!

Vista Peak Options

Vista Peak is only 0.5 mile north of Mount Solitude and is a nice ridge walk. It's possible to descend Vista's west slopes into one basin north of the Solitude Basin and regain the Pitkin Creek Trail there—the slope terrain is the same stuff, Class 2 grassy hills with embedded rocks.

This slope is also a possible ascent route. Stay on the Pitkin Creek Trail 0.6 mile farther from the split to Solitude Basin and then leave the trail and go up Vista's western slopes. Traverse the ridge to the Climbers/Skiers Point saddle and drop down there. The mileage for this route is about 12.9 miles—a big day, but remember the on-trail portions will go quickly.

Hiking legend Sopris the mountain dog with Vista Peak on the right and Mount Solitude on the left

photographed by Jon Bradford

The locals pay a visit. Mountain goats are a common
sight in the Gore Range (see page 158).

Afterword

In my notes for this book, the final entry reads:

"Done east to west, these hikes turn boys into men. Girls into women. Puppies into dogs. You get the idea."

It is by wonderful coincidence that the mountains along I-70 offer an organic progression of routes that culminate in the wonderful, challenging, and remote Gore Range. Starting with the gentle slopes of Mount Bancroft, an aspiring mountain hiker will graduate to the thrilling exposure of Kelso Ridge, navigate the difficult west ridge of Pacific Peak, and finally master the Valhalla–Snow Peak traverse above Deluge Lake. Hikers who complete these adventures will be left tempted and yearning, pondering the deeper-still reaches of the Gore Range. The sequel is theirs to write.

In the three years it took to develop this book, I've come to realize that the destinations in this guide transcend convenience or compromise; they are some of the most enjoyable and adventurous peaks in Colorado. Just because they happen to be a modest drive from the Denver metro area, do not be fooled into thinking that these mountains are less visited because they are subpar adventures. As I peruse my photos, I see the dramatic cliffs of Witter Peak, the secret garden above Fall River Reservoir, the moving panoramas below Peak 6, and the unrivaled aspects from the summit of Jacque Peak—all of them stir the soul, and none of them were in the script to create lasting memories before I visited them.

Peel the objective data back a layer, and therein is the heart of this book. It is not lost on me that, if this guide is successful, it serves as a catalyst to the story of your own adventure. What I remember are powerful conversations among friends, the boundless enthusiasm of my dogs, the dumbfounding beauty of neglected ridgelines, the terrifying storms that sent me scurrying, and most of all, the sense of incredible gratitude to live in such a glorious place.

Besides earning my rank as a mobile know-it-all when pointing out the summits along I-70, I've developed a deeper appreciation for just how good we have it in Colorado. I can't begin to define what intangible hunger is satisfied by being in the mountains, but there is no doubt in my mind that the call to wilderness is driven by an essential curiosity that often remains unexpressed in the comparatively dull and predictable front country.

I'd bet a can of Alpo that my dogs feel the same way.

One final thought: On the summit of Point 12,805, I happened to catch a particularly glorious sunset in the company of my dogs, Mystic and Fremont. The city lights of Silverthorne began to shine in the warm twilight, and the crawling I-70 traffic fused into a single, glowing serpent twisting through the valley below. High above, the three of us watched it all as if we were exempt from the orchestrated dictates of both nature and society.

But night was falling, and friends were waiting; it was time to go.

I would have thought the airy feeling of transcendence would be lost in the noise of emotions that make up the memory of an adventure, but thankfully that moment remains vivid in my mind. Some nights while I fade to sleep, it drifts into my semiconscious thoughts. There, on an obscure, overlooked mountain, I was treated to a rare glimpse of how utterly beautiful it is to walk upon this Earth.

That our foot- and paw prints were soon to be swept away was of no importance.

Appendix 1: Peaks by Elevation

Peak	Elevation
1. Grays Peak	14,270'
2. Torreys Peak	14,267'
3. Fletcher Mountain	13,951'
4. Pacific Peak	13,950'
5. Drift Peak	13,900'
6. Crystal Peak	13,852'
7. Mount Edwards	13,850'
8. Atlantic Peak	13,841'
9. Argentine Peak	13,738'
10. Bard Peak	13,641'
11. Peak 10	13,633'
12. Father Dyer Peak	13,615'
13. McClellan Mountain	13,587'
14. Mount Parnassus	13,574'
15. Pettingell Peak	13,553'
16. Grizzly Peak	13,427'
17. Point 13,418	13,418'
18. Mount Wilcox	13,408'
19. Parry Peak	13,391'
20. Engelmann Peak	13,362'
21. The Citadel	13,294'
22. James Peak	13,294'
23. Mount Bancroft	13,250'
24. Peak 6	13,250'
25. Mount Sniktau	13,234'
26. Hagar Mountain	13,220'
27. Jacque Peak	13,205'
28. Lenawee Peak	13,204'
29. Red Peak	13,189'
30. Mount Valhalla	13,180'
31. Kelso Mountain	13,164'
32. Robeson Peak	13,141'
33. Grand Traverse Peak	13,140'
34. Mount Flora	13,132'
35. Mount Eva	13,130'
36. "Cupid" Peak	13,117'
37. Mount Solitude	13,090'
38. Vista Peak	13,075'
39. Snow Peak	13,024'
40. "Golden Bear Peak"	13,010'
41. Climbers Point	13,005'
42. Peak 8	12,987'
43. Woods Mountain	12,940'
44. Tenmile Peak	12,933'
45. Loveland Mountain	12,930'
46. Deming Mountain	12,902'
47. Ganley Mountain	12,902'
48. Breckenridge Peak	12,889'
49. Mount Eva	12,889'
50. Witter Peak	12,884'
51. Peak 4	12,866'
52. Peak 5	12,855'
53. UN 12,805	12,805'
54. Peak 1	12,805'
55. Buffalo Mountain	12,777'
56. Otter Mountain	12,766'
57. Coon Hill	12,757'
58. Sacred Buffalo	12,755'

Peak	Elevation
59. Loveland Continental Divide	12,752'
60. West Deming Peak	12,736'
61. UN 12,716	12,716'
62. Mount Bethel	12,705'
63. "Lonely Ridge" high point	12,700'
64. Peak 3	12,676'
65. UN 12,671	12,671'
66. Peak 7	12,665'
67. Skiers Point	12,620'
68. Peak 6	12,573'
69. Uneva Peak	12,522'
70. Sugarloaf Peak	12,513'
71. Ptarmigan Peak	12,498'
72. Mount Trelease	12,477'
73. Silver Plume Mountain	12,477'
74. Baker Mountain	12,448'
75. Copper Mountain	12,441'
76. UN 12,438	12,438'
77. Peak 6.5	12,438'

Peak	Elevation
78. UN 12,414	12,414'
79. Mayflower Hill	12,388'
80. Republican Mountain	12,386'
81. Point 12,363	12,363'
82. Eccles Peak	12,313'
83. Union Mountain	12,313'
84. Sherman Mountain	12,287'
85. Pendleton Mountain	12,275'
86. Sneva Peak	12,242'
87. UN 12,212	12,212'
88. Kingston Peak	12,147'
89. Wingle Ridge	11,977'
90. Shrine Mountain	11,888'
91. Griffith Mountain	11,568'
92. Alpine Peak	11,552'
93. Tenderfoot Mountain	11,441'
94. Independence Mountain	11,440'
95. Royal Mountain	10,502'

Appendix 2: Contact Information

Arapaho National Forest
Clear Creek Ranger District
www.fs.usda.gov/arp
101 CO 103
Idaho Springs, CO 80452
303-567-3000

Arapaho National Forest
Sulphur Ranger District
www.fs.usda.gov/arp
9 Ten Mile Drive
Granby, CO 80446
970-887-4100

White River National Forest (West of Vail Pass)
www.fs.usda.gov/whiteriver
900 Grand Ave.
Glenwood Springs, CO 81601
970-945-2521

Eagles Nest Wilderness
Dillon Ranger District
www.fs.usda.gov/whiteriver
680 Blue River Pkwy.
Silverthorne, CO 80498
970-468-5400

Loveland Ski Area
skiloveland.com
303-571-5580
I-70, Exit 216

Appendix 3: Additional Resources

Emergency Veterinarian Services Along I-70

Frisco Animal Hospital (24/7 Emergency Care)
700 N. Summit Blvd.
Frisco, CO 80443
970-368-5059
friscoanimalhospital.com

Vail Valley Animal Hospital, Edwards (24/7 Emergency Care)
105 Edwards Village Blvd., Ste. 101 A & B
Edwards, CO 81632
970-926-3496
970-949-4044 (emergency number)
vailvalleyanimalhospital.com

Vail Valley Animal Hospital, Eagle-Vail
40843 US 6
Avon, CO 81620
970-949-4044
vailvalleyanimalhospital.com

Gear Shops Along I-70

Clear Creek Outdoors
1524 Miner St.
Idaho Springs, CO 80452
303-567-1500
clearcreekoutdoors.com

Wilderness Sports
701 E. Anemone Trail
Dillon, CO 80435
970-468-5687
wildernesssports.com

Marmot Vail
288 Bridge St., Unit 2
Vail, CO 81657
970-306-0675
marmot.com

Appendix 4: **Online Resources**

summitpost.org
An excellent collection of information on summit hikes. Some information may be outdated as it is user maintained, but still highly recommended.
summitpost.org

14ers.com
Not just great info on the fourteeners (of which there are only two in this guide) but also thirteeners (of which there are many).
14ers.com

Mountainous Words
The author's website offers free GPX or KMZ files for download.
mountainouswords.com/I70-hikes

Index